JAPANESE

VOCABULARY

FOR ENGLISH SPEAKERS

ENGLISH-JAPANESE

The most useful words
To expand your lexicon and sharpen
your language skills

7000 words

This "book of new words" will be your personal, unique list of words. However, it will only contain the words that you came across during the learning process. For example, you might have written down the words "Sunday," "Tuesday," and "Friday." However, there are additional words for days of the week, for example, "Saturday," that are missing, and your list of words would be incomplete. Using a theme dictionary, in addition to the "book of new words," is a reasonable solution to this problem.

You're welcome	どういたしまして	dōitashimashite
Don't mention it!	礼なんていいよ	rei nante ī yo
It was nothing	どういたしまして	dōitashimashite
Excuse me! (fam.)	失礼！	shitsurei!
Excuse me! (form.)	失礼致します！	shitsurei itashi masu!
to excuse (forgive)	許す	yurusu
to apologize (vi)	謝る	ayamaru
My apologies	おわび致します！	owabi itashi masu!
I'm sorry!	ごめんなさい！	gomennasai!
to forgive (vt)	許す	yurusu
It's okay!	大丈夫です！	daijōbu desu!
please (adv)	お願い	onegai
Don't forget!	忘れないで！	wasure nai de!
Certainly!	もちろん！	mochiron!
Of course not!	そんなことないよ！	sonna koto nai yo!
Okay! (I agree)	オーケー！	ōkē!
That's enough!	もう十分だ！	mō jūbun da!

3.

23 twenty-three	二十三	ni jū san
30 thirty	三十	san jū
31 thirty-one	三一	san jū ichi
32 thirty-two	三二	san jū ni
33 thirty-three	三三	san jū san
40 forty	四十	yon jū
41 forty-one	四一	yon jū ichi
42 forty-two	四二	yon jū ni
43 forty-three	四三	yon jū san
50 fifty	五十	go jū
51 fifty-one	五十一	go jū ichi
52 fifty-two	五十二	go jū ni
53 fifty-three	五十三	go jū san
60 sixty	六十	roku jū
61 sixty-one	六十一	roku jū ichi
62 sixty-two	六十二	roku jū ni
63 sixty-three	六十三	roku jū san
70 seventy	七十	nana jū
71 seventy-one	七十一	nana jū ichi
72 seventy-two	七十二	nana jū ni
73 seventy-three	七十三	nana jū san
80 eighty	八十	hachi jū
81 eighty-one	八十一	hachi jū ichi
82 eighty-two	八十二	hachi jū ni
83 eighty-three	八十三	hachi jū san
90 ninety	九十	kyū jū
91 ninety-one	九十一	kyū jū ichi
92 ninety-two	九十二	kyū jū ni
93 ninety-three	九十三	kyū jū san

4.

3000 three thousand	三千	sanzen
10000 ten thousand	一万	ichiman
one hundred thousand	10万	jyūman
million	百万	hyakuman
billion	十億	jūoku

5.

How many?	いくつ？	ikutsu ?
sum, total	合計	gōkei
result	結果	kekka
remainder	剰余、余り	jōyo, amari
a few ...	少数の	shōsū no
few, little (adv)	少し	sukoshi
the rest	残り	nokori
one and a half	1,5	ittengo
dozen	ダース	dāsu
in half (adv)	半分に	hanbun ni
equally (evenly)	均等に	kintō ni
half	半分	hanbun
time (three ~s)	回	kai

8.

to continue (vt)	続ける	tsuzukeru
to control (vt)	管制する	kansei suru
to cook (dinner)	料理をする	ryōri wo suru
to cost (vt)	かかる	kakaru
to count (add up)	計算する	keisan suru
to count on ...	…を頼りにする	... wo tayori ni suru
to create (vt)	創造する	sōzō suru
to cry (weep)	泣く	naku

9.

to hide (vt)	隠す	kakusu
to hope (vi, vt)	希望する	kibō suru
to hunt (vi, vt)	狩る	karu
to hurry (vi)	急ぐ	isogu

10.

to punish (vt)	罰する	bassuru
to read (vi, vt)	読む	yomu
to recommend (vt)	推薦する	suisen suru
to refuse (vi, vt)	拒絶する	kyozetsu suru
to regret (be sorry)	後悔する	kōkai suru
to rent (sth from sb)	借りる	kariru
to repeat (say again)	復唱する	fukushō suru
to reserve, to book	予約する	yoyaku suru
to run (vi)	走る	hashiru

11.

to warn (vt)	警告する	keikoku suru
to work (vi)	働く	hataraku
to write (vt)	書く	kaku
to write down	書き留める	kakitomeru

12.

13.

left (adj)	左の	hidari no
on the left	左に	hidari ni
to the left	左へ	hidari he
right (adj)	右の	migi no
on the right	右に	migi ni
to the right	右へ	migi he
in front (adv)	前に	mae ni
front (as adj)	前の	mae no
ahead (look ~)	前方へ	zenpō he
behind (adv)	後ろに	ushiro ni
from behind	後ろから	ushiro kara
back (towards the rear)	後ろへ	ushiro he
middle	中央	chūō
in the middle	中央に	chūō ni
at the side	側面から	sokumen kara
everywhere (adv)	どこでも	doko demo
around (in all directions)	…の周りを	… no mawari wo
from inside	中から	naka kara
somewhere (to go)	どこかへ	dokoka he
straight (directly)	真っ直ぐに	massugu ni
back (e.g., come ~)	戻って	modotte
from anywhere	どこからでも	doko kara demo
from somewhere	どこからか	doko kara ka
firstly (adv)	第一に	dai ichi ni
secondly (adv)	第二に	dai ni ni
thirdly (adv)	第三に	dai san ni
suddenly (adv)	急に	kyū ni
at first (adv)	初めは	hajime wa
for the first time	初めて	hajimete
long before …	…かなり前に	…kanari mae ni
anew (over again)	新たに	arata ni
for good (adv)	永遠に	eien ni
never (adv)	一度も	ichi do mo
again (adv)	再び	futatabi
now (adv)	今	ima
often (adv)	よく	yoku
then (adv)	あのとき	ano toki
urgently (quickly)	至急に	shikyū ni
usually (adv)	普通は	futsū wa
by the way, …	ところで、…	tokorode, …
possible (that is ~)	可能な	kanō na

probably (adv)	恐らく［おそらく］	osoraku
maybe (adv)	ことによると	kotoni yoru to
besides ...	それに	soreni
that's why ...	従って	shitagatte
in spite of ...	…にもかかわらず	... ni mo kakawara zu
thanks to ...	…のおかげで	... no okage de
what (pron.)	何	nani
that (conj.)	…ということ	... toyuu koto
something	何か	nani ka
anything (something)	何か	nani ka
nothing	何もない	nani mo nai
who (pron.)	誰	dare
someone	ある人	aru hito
somebody	誰か	dare ka
nobody	誰も…ない	dare mo ... nai
nowhere (a voyage to ~)	どこへも	doko he mo
nobody's	誰の…でもない	dare no ... de mo nai
somebody's	誰かの	dare ka no
so (I'm ~ glad)	とても	totemo
also (as well)	また	mata
too (as well)	も	mo

15.

each (adj)	各	kaku
any (no matter which)	どれでも	dore demo
many (adv)	多くの	ōku no
much (adv)	多量の	taryō no
many people	多くの人々	ōku no hitobito
all (everyone)	あらゆる人	arayuru hito
in return for …	…の返礼として	… no henrei toshite
in exchange (adv)	引き換えに	hikikae ni
by hand (made)	手で	te de
hardly (negative opinion)	ほとんど…ない	hotondo … nai
probably (adv)	恐らく［おそらく］	osoraku
on purpose (adv)	わざと	wazato
by accident (adv)	偶然に	gūzen ni
very (adv)	非常に	hijō ni
for example (adv)	例えば	tatoeba
between	間	kan
among	…の間で	… no мade
so much (such a lot)	たくさん	takusan
especially (adv)	特に	tokuni

in the afternoon	午後に	gogo ni
evening	夕方	yūgata
in the evening	夕方に	yūgata ni
night	夜	yoru
at night	夜に	yoru ni
midnight	真夜中	mayonaka
second	秒	byō
minute	分	fun, pun
hour	時間	jikan
half an hour	30分	san jū fun
quarter of an hour	15分	jū go fun
fifteen minutes	15分	jū go fun
24 hours	一昼夜	icchūya
sunrise	日の出	hinode
dawn	夜明け	yoake
early morning	早朝	sōchō
sunset	夕日	yūhi
early in the morning	早朝に	sōchō ni
this morning	今朝	kesa
tomorrow morning	明日の朝	ashita no asa
this afternoon	今日の午後	kyō no gogo
in the afternoon	午後	gogo
tomorrow afternoon	明日の午後	ashita no gogo
tonight (this evening)	今夜	konya
tomorrow night	明日の夜	ashita no yoru
at 3 o'clock sharp	3時ちょうどに	sanji chōdo ni
about 4 o'clock	4時頃	yoji goro
by 12 o'clock	12時までに	jūniji made ni
in 20 minutes	20分後	nijuppungo
in an hour	一時間後	ichi jikan go
on time (adv)	予定通りに	yotei dōri ni
a quarter of ...	…時15分	... ji jyūgo fun
within an hour	1時間で	ichi jikan de
every 15 minutes	15分ごとに	jyūgo fun goto ni
round the clock	昼も夜も	hiru mo yoru mo

18.

May	五月	gogatsu
June	六月	rokugatsu
July	七月	shichigatsu
August	八月	hachigatsu
September	九月	kugatsu
October	十月	jūgatsu
November	十一月	jūichigatsu
December	十二月	jūnigatsu
spring	春	haru
in spring	春に	haru ni
spring (as adj)	春の	haru no
summer	夏	natsu
in summer	夏に	natsu ni
summer (as adj)	夏の	natsu no
fall	秋	aki
in fall	秋に	aki ni
fall (as adj)	秋の	aki no
winter	冬	fuyu
in winter	冬に	fuyu ni
winter (as adj)	冬の	fuyu no
month	月	tsuki
this month	今月	kongetsu
next month	来月	raigetsu
last month	先月	sengetsu
a month ago	一ヶ月前	ichi kagetsu mae
in a month	一ヶ月後	ichi kagetsu go
in two months	二ヶ月後	ni kagetsu go
the whole month	丸一ヶ月	maru ichi kagetsu
all month long	一ヶ月間ずっと	ichi kagetsu kan zutto
monthly (~ magazine)	月刊の	gekkan no
monthly (adv)	毎月	maitsuki
every month	月1回	tsuki ichi kai
twice a month	月に2回	tsuki ni ni kai
year	年	nen
this year	今年	kotoshi
next year	来年	rainen
last year	去年	kyonen
a year ago	一年前	ichi nen mae
in a year	一年後	ichi nen go
in two years	二年後	ni nen go
the whole year	丸一年	maru ichi nen
all year long	通年	tsūnen

every year	毎年	maitoshi
annual (adj)	毎年の	maitoshi no
annually (adv)	年1回	toshi ichi kai
4 times a year	年に4回	
date (e.g., today's ~)	日付	hizuke
date (e.g., ~ of birth)	年月日	nengappi
calendar	カレンダー	karendā
half a year	半年	hantoshi
six months	6ヶ月	
season (summer, etc.)	季節	kisetsu
century	世紀	seiki

19.

memories (childhood ~)	思い出	omoide
archives	公文書	kōbunsho
during …	間に	aida ni
long, a long time (adv)	長く	nagaku
not long (adv)	長くない	nagaku nai
early (in the morning)	早く	hayaku
late (not early)	遅くに	osoku ni
forever (for good)	永遠に	eien ni
to start (begin)	始める	hajimeru
to postpone (vt)	延期する	enki suru
at the same time	同時に	dōjini
permanently (adv)	不変に	fuhen ni
constant (noise, pain)	絶えず続く	taezu tsuzuku
temporary (adj)	一時的な	ichiji teki na
sometimes (adv)	時々	tokidoki
rarely (adv)	まれに	mare ni
often (adv)	よく	yoku

20.

deep (adj)	深い	fukai
shallow (adj)	浅い	asai
yes	はい	hai
no	いいえ	īe
distant (in space)	遠くの	tōku no
nearby (adj)	近くの	chikaku no
far (adv)	遠くに	tōku ni
nearby (adv)	近くに	chikaku ni
long (adj)	長い	nagai
short (adj)	短い	mijikai
good (kindhearted)	良い	yoi
evil (adj)	悪い	warui
married (adj)	既婚の	kikon no
single (adj)	独身の	dokushin no
to forbid (vt)	禁じる	kinjiru
to permit (vt)	許可する	kyoka suru
end	最後	saigo
beginning	最初	saisho
left (adj)	左の	hidari no
right (adj)	右の	migi no
first (adj)	第一の	dai ichi no
last (adj)	最後の	saigo no
crime	罪	tsumi
punishment	罰	batsu
to order (vt)	命令する	meirei suru
to obey (vi, vt)	従う	shitagau
straight (adj)	直…、真っすぐな	choku ..., massuguna
curved (adj)	曲がった	magatta
paradise	極楽	gokuraku
hell	地獄	jigoku
to be born	生まれる	umareru
to die (vi)	死ぬ	shinu
strong (adj)	強い	tsuyoi
weak (adj)	弱い	yowai
old (adj)	年上の	toshiue no
young (adj)	若い	wakai

old (adj)	古い	furui
new (adj)	新しい	atarashī
hard (adj)	硬い	katai
soft (adj)	柔らかい	yawarakai
warm (adj)	暖かい	atatakai
cold (adj)	寒い	samui
fat (adj)	でぶの	debu no
thin (adj)	痩せた	yase ta
narrow (adj)	狭い	semai
wide (adj)	広い	hiroi
good (adj)	良い	yoi
bad (adj)	悪い	warui
brave (adj)	勇敢な	yūkan na
cowardly (adj)	臆病な	okubyō na

21.

parallel (n)	平行	heikō
parallel (as adj)	平行の	heikō no
line	線	sen
stroke	一画	ikkaku
straight line	直線	chokusen
curve (curved line)	曲線	kyokusen
thin (line, etc.)	細い	hosoi
contour (outline)	輪郭	rinkaku
intersection	交点	kōten
right angle	直角	chokkaku
segment	弓形	kyūkei
sector	扇形	senkei
side (of triangle)	辺	hen
angle	角	kaku

22.

ampere	アンペア	anpea
horsepower	馬力	bariki
quantity	数量	sūryō
a little bit of ...	少し	sukoshi
half	半分	hanbun
dozen	ダース	dāsu
piece (item)	一個	ikko
size	大きさ	ōki sa
scale (map ~)	縮尺	shukushaku
minimal (adj)	極小の	kyokushō no
the smallest (adj)	最小の	saishō no
medium (adj)	中位の	chūi no
maximal (adj)	極大の	kyokudai no
the largest (adj)	最大の	saidai no

23.

tube (of toothpaste)	チューブ	chūbu
sack (bag)	南京袋	nankinbukuro
bag (paper ~, plastic ~)	袋	fukuro
pack (of cigarettes, etc.)	箱	hako
box (e.g., shoebox)	箱	hako
crate	木箱	ki bako
basket	かご［籠］	kago

24.

25.

triceps	三頭筋	san tō suji
tendon	腱	ken
joint	関節	kansetsu
lungs	肺	hai
genitals	生殖器	seishoku ki
skin	肌	hada

28.

red-haired (adj)	赤毛の	akage no
gray (hair)	白髪の	hakuhatsu no
bald (adj)	はげ頭の	hageatama no
bald patch	はげた部分	hage ta bubun
ponytail	ポニーテール	ponītēru
bangs	前髪	maegami

29.

workwear	作業服	sagyō fuku
overalls	オーバーオール	ōbā ōru
coat (e.g., doctor's smock)	コート	kōto

32.

boots (cowboy ~)	ブーツ	būtsu
slippers	スリッパ	surippa
tennis shoes	テニスシューズ	tenisu shūzu
sneakers	スニーカー	sunīkā
sandals	サンダル	sandaru
cobbler	靴修理屋	kutsu shūri ya
heel	かかと［踵］	kakato
pair (of shoes)	靴一足	kutsu issoku
shoestring	靴ひも	kutsu himo
to lace (vt)	靴ひもを結ぶ	kutsu himo wo musubu
shoehorn	靴べら	kutsubera
shoe polish	靴クリーム	kutsu kurīmu

35.

frame (eyeglass ~)	めがねのふち	megane no fuchi
umbrella	傘	kasa
walking stick	杖	tsue
hairbrush	ヘアブラシ	hea burashi
fan	扇子	sensu
necktie	ネクタイ	nekutai
bow tie	蝶ネクタイ	chō nekutai
suspenders	サスペンダー	sasupendā
handkerchief	ハンカチ	hankachi
comb	くし［櫛］	kushi
barrette	髪留め	kami tome
hairpin	ヘアピン	hea pin
buckle	バックル	bakkuru
belt	ベルト	beruto
shoulder strap	ショルダーベルト	shorudā beruto
bag (handbag)	バッグ	baggu
purse	ハンドバッグ	hando baggu
backpack	バックパック	bakku pakku

37.

to crease, crumple (vi)	しわになる	shiwa ni naru
to tear (vt)	引き裂く	hikisaku
clothes moth	コイガ	koi ga

38.

anti-wrinkle cream	しわ取りクリーム	shiwa tori kurīmu
day cream	昼用クリーム	hiruyō kurīmu
night cream	夜用クリーム	yoruyō kurīmu
day (as adj)	昼用…	hiruyō …
night (as adj)	夜用…	yoruyō …
tampon	タンポン	tanpon
toilet paper	トイレットペーパー	toiretto pēpā
hair dryer	ヘアドライヤー	hea doraiyā

39.

sundial	日時計	hidokei
alarm clock	目覚まし時計	mezamashi dokei
watchmaker	時計職人	tokei shokunin
to repair (vt)	修理する	shūri suru

salmon	サケ [鮭]	sake
halibut	ハリバット	haribatto
cod	タラ [鱈]	tara
mackerel	サバ [鯖]	saba
tuna	マグロ [鮪]	maguro
eel	ウナギ [鰻]	unagi
trout	マス [鱒]	masu
sardine	イワシ	iwashi
pike	カワカマス	kawakamasu
herring	ニシン	nishin
bread	パン	pan
cheese	チーズ	chīzu
sugar	砂糖	satō
salt	塩	shio
rice	米	kome
pasta	パスタ	pasuta
noodles	麺	men
butter	バター	batā
vegetable oil	植物油	shokubutsu yu
sunflower oil	ひまわり油	himawari yu
margarine	マーガリン	māgarin
olives	オリーブ	orību
olive oil	オリーブ油	orību yu
milk	乳、ミルク	nyū, miruku
condensed milk	練乳	rennyū
yogurt	ヨーグルト	yōguruto
sour cream	サワークリーム	sawā kurīmu
cream (of milk)	クリーム	kurīmu
mayonnaise	マヨネーズ	mayonēzu
buttercream	バタークリーム	batā kurīmu
cereal grain (wheat, etc.)	穀物	kokumotsu
flour	小麦粉	komugiko
canned food	缶詰	kanzume
cornflakes	コーンフレーク	kōn furēku
honey	蜂蜜	hachimitsu
jam	ジャム	jamu
chewing gum	チューインガム	chūin gamu

42.

still (adj)	無炭酸の	mu tansan no
carbonated (adj)	炭酸の	tansan no
sparkling (adj)	発泡性の	happō sei no
ice	氷	kōri
with ice	氷入りの	kōri iri no
non-alcoholic (adj)	ノンアルコールの	non arukŌru no
soft drink	炭酸飲料	tansan inryō
cool soft drink	清涼飲料水	seiryōinryōsui
lemonade	レモネード	remonēdo
liquor	アルコール	arukōru
wine	ワイン	wain
white wine	白ワイン	shiro wain
red wine	赤ワイン	aka wain
liqueur	リキュール	rikyūru
champagne	シャンパン	shanpan
vermouth	ベルモット	berumotto
whisky	ウイスキー	uisukī
vodka	ウォッカ	wokka
gin	ジン	jin
cognac	コニャック	konyakku
rum	ラム酒	ramu shu
coffee	コーヒー	kōhī
black coffee	ブラックコーヒー	burakku kōhī
coffee with milk	ミルク入りコーヒー	miruku iri kōhī
cappuccino	カプチーノ	kapuchīno
instant coffee	インスタントコーヒー	insutanto kōhī
milk	乳、ミルク	nyū, miruku
cocktail	カクテル	kakuteru
milk shake	ミルクセーキ	miruku sēki
juice	ジュース	jūsu
tomato juice	トマトジュース	tomato jūsu
orange juice	オレンジジュース	orenji jūsu
freshly squeezed juice	搾りたてのジュース	shibori tate no jūsu
beer	ビール	bīru
light beer	ライトビール	raito bīru
dark beer	黒ビール	kuro bīru
tea	茶	cha
black tea	紅茶	kō cha
green tea	緑茶	ryoku cha

43.

peach	モモ［桃］	momo
apricot	アンズ［杏子］	anzu
raspberry	ラズベリー（木苺）	razuberī
pineapple	パイナップル	painappuru
banana	バナナ	banana
watermelon	スイカ	suika
grape	ブドウ［葡萄］	budō
cherry	チェリー	cherī
sour cherry	サワー チェリー	sawā cherī
sweet cherry	スイート チェリー	suīto cherī
melon	メロン	meron
grapefruit	グレープフルーツ	gurēbu furūtsu
avocado	アボカド	abokado
papaya	パパイヤ	papaiya
mango	マンゴー	mangō
pomegranate	ザクロ	zakuro
redcurrant	フサスグリ	fusa suguri
blackcurrant	クロスグリ	kuro suguri
gooseberry	セイヨウスグリ	seiyō suguri
bilberry	ビルベリー	biruberī
blackberry	ブラックベリー	burakku berī
raisin	レーズン	rēzun
fig	イチジク	ichijiku
date	デーツ	dētsu
peanut	ピーナッツ	pīnattsu
almond	アーモンド	āmondo
walnut	クルミ（胡桃）	kurumi
hazelnut	ヘーゼルナッツ	hēzeru nattsu
coconut	ココナッツ	koko nattsu
pistachios	ピスタチオ	pisutachio

45.

whole fruit jam	ジャム	jamu
marmalade	マーマレード	māmarēdo
waffle	ワッフル	waffuru
ice-cream	アイスクリーム	aisukurīmu
pudding	プディング	pudingu

46.

to salt (vt)	塩をかける	shio wo kakeru
to pepper (vt)	コショウをかける	koshō wo kakeru
to grate (vt)	すりおろす	suri orosu
peel (n)	皮	kawa
to peel (vt)	皮をむく	kawa wo muku

47.

to open (~ a bottle)	開ける	akeru
to spill (liquid)	こぼす	kobosu
to spill out (vi)	こぼれる	koboreru

to boil (vi)	沸く	waku
to boil (vt)	沸かす	wakasu
boiled (~ water)	沸騰させた	futtō sase ta
to chill, cool down (vt)	冷やす	hiyasu
to chill (vi)	冷える	hieru

taste, flavor	味	aji
aftertaste	後味	atoaji

to be on a diet	ダイエットをする	daietto wo suru
diet	ダイエット	daietto
vitamin	ビタミン	bitamin
calorie	カロリー	karorī
vegetarian (n)	ベジタリアン	bejitarian
vegetarian (adj)	ベジタリアン用の	bejitarian yōno

fats (nutrient)	脂肪	shibō
proteins	タンパク質［蛋白質］	tanpaku shitsu
carbohydrates	炭水化物	tansuikabutsu
slice (of lemon, ham)	スライス	suraisu
piece (of cake, pie)	一切れ	ichi kire
crumb (of bread)	くず	kuzu

49.

bartender	バーテンダー	bātendā
menu	メニュー	menyū
wine list	ワインリスト	wain risuto
to book a table	テーブルを予約する	tēburu wo yoyaku suru
course, dish	料理	ryōri
to order (meal)	注文する	chūmon suru
to make an order	注文する	chūmon suru
aperitif	アペリティフ	aperitifu
appetizer	前菜	zensai
dessert	デザート	dezāto
check	お勘定	okanjō
to pay the check	勘定を払う	kanjō wo harau
to give change	釣り銭を渡す	tsurisen wo watasu
tip	チップ	chippu

grandmother	祖母	sobo
grandfather	祖父	sofu
grandson	孫息子	mago musuko
granddaughter	孫娘	mago musume
grandchildren	孫	mago
uncle	伯父	oji
aunt	伯母	oba
nephew	甥	oi
niece	姪	mei
mother-in-law (wife's mother)	妻の母親	tsuma no hahaoya
father-in-law (husband's father)	義父	gifu
son-in-law (daughter's husband)	娘の夫	musume no otto
stepmother	継母	keibo
stepfather	継父	keifu
infant	乳児	nyūji
baby (infant)	赤ん坊	akanbō
little boy, kid	子供	kodomo
wife	妻	tsuma
husband	夫	otto
spouse (husband)	配偶者	haigū sha
spouse (wife)	配偶者	haigū sha
married (masc.)	既婚の	kikon no
married (fem.)	既婚の	kikon no
single (unmarried)	独身の	dokushin no
bachelor	独身男性	dokushin dansei
divorced (masc.)	離婚した	rikon shi ta
widow	未亡人	mibōjin
widower	男やもめ	otokoyamome
relative	親戚	shinseki
close relative	近い親戚	chikai shinseki
distant relative	遠い親戚	tōi shinseki
relatives	親族	shinzoku
orphan (boy or girl)	孤児	koji
guardian (of minor)	後見人	kōkennin
to adopt (a boy)	養子にする	yōshi ni suru
to adopt (a girl)	養女にする	yōjo ni suru

53.

friendship	友情	yūjō
to be friends	友達だ	tomodachi da
buddy (masc.)	友達	tomodachi
buddy (fem.)	女友達	onna tomodachi
partner	パートナー	pātonā
chief (boss)	長	chō
superior	上司、上役	jōshi, uwayaku
owner, proprietor	経営者	keieisha
subordinate	部下	buka
colleague	同僚	dōryō
acquaintance (person)	知り合い	shiriai
fellow traveler	同調者	dōchō sha
classmate	クラスメート	kurasumēto
neighbor (masc.)	隣人、近所	rinjin, kinjo
neighbor (fem.)	隣人、近所	rinjin, kinjo
neighbors	隣人	rinjin

54.

stout, fat (adj)	太った	futotta
swarthy (adj)	小麦肌の	komugi hada no
well-built (adj)	マッチョの	maccho no
elegant (adj)	上品な	jōhin na

55.

construction set	組み立ておもちゃ	kumitate omocha
well-bred (adj)	育ちの良い	sodachi no yoi
ill-bred (adj)	育ちの悪い	sodachi no warui
spoiled (adj)	甘やかされた	amayakasare ta
to be naughty	悪戯をする	itazura wo suru
mischievous (adj)	悪戯好きな	itazura zuki na
mischievousness	悪戯	itazura
mischievous child	悪戯っ子	itazurakko
obedient (adj)	従順な	jūjun na
disobedient (adj)	反抗的な	hankō teki na
docile (adj)	大人しい	otonashī
clever (smart)	利口な	rikō na
child prodigy	神童	shindō

57.

anniversary	記念日	kinen bi
lover (masc.)	恋人	koibito
mistress	愛人	aijin
adultery	不倫	furin
to cheat on ... (commit adultery)	不倫する	furin suru
jealous (adj)	焼きもち焼きの	yakimochi yaki no
to be jealous	焼きもちを焼く	yakimochi wo yaku
divorce	離婚	rikon
to divorce (vi)	離婚する	rikon suru
to quarrel (vi)	口論する	kōron suru
to be reconciled	仲直りする	nakanaori suru
together (adv)	一緒に	issho ni
sex	セックス	sekkusu
happiness	幸福	kōfuku
happy (adj)	幸福な	kōfuku na
misfortune (accident)	不幸	fukō
unhappy (adj)	不幸な	fukō na

fury (madness)	憤激	fungeki
rage (fury)	激怒	gekido
depression	落ち込み	ochikomi
discomfort	不快感	fukai kan
comfort	心地よさ	kokochiyo sa
to regret (be sorry)	後悔する	kōkai suru
regret	後悔	kōkai
bad luck	不運	fuun
sadness	悲しさ	kanashi sa
shame (remorse)	恥	haji
gladness	喜び	yorokobi
enthusiasm, zeal	熱意	netsui
enthusiast	熱意を持っている人	netsui wo motte iru hito
to show enthusiasm	熱意を示す	netsui wo shimesu

59.

talent	才能	sainō
courageous (adj)	勇敢な	yūkan na
courage	勇敢さ	yūkan sa
honest (adj)	正直な	shōjiki na
honesty	正直	shōjiki
careful (cautious)	用心して	yōjin shi te
brave (courageous)	勇ましい	isamashī
serious (adj)	真剣な	shinken na
strict (severe, stern)	厳しい	kibishī
decisive (adj)	決断力のある	ketsudan ryoku no aru
indecisive (adj)	優柔不断な	yūjūfudan na
shy, timid (adj)	内気な	uchiki na
shyness, timidity	内気	uchiki
confidence (trust)	信用	shinyō
to believe (trust)	信用する	shinyō suru
trusting (naïve)	信じやすい	shinji yasui
sincerely (adv)	心から	kokorokara
sincere (adj)	心からの	kokorokara no
sincerity	誠実	seijitsu
open (person)	率直な	socchoku na
calm (adj)	平静な	heisei na
frank (sincere)	正直な	shōjiki na
naïve (adj)	うぶな	ubu na
absent-minded (adj)	上の空な	uwanosora na
funny (odd)	おかしな	okashina
greed	欲張り	yokubari
greedy (adj)	欲張りの	yokubari no
stingy (adj)	けちな	kechi na
evil (adj)	悪い	warui
stubborn (adj)	頑固な	ganko na
unpleasant (adj)	感じの悪い	kanji no warui
selfish person (masc.)	わがまま	wagamama
selfish (adj)	わがままな	wagamama na
coward	臆病者	okubyō mono
cowardly (adj)	臆病な	okubyō na

60.

bed	ベッド、寝台	beddo, shindai
mattress	マットレス	mattoresu
blanket (comforter)	毛布	mōfu
pillow	枕	makura
sheet	シーツ、敷布	shītsu, shikifu
insomnia	不眠症	fuminshō
sleepless (adj)	眠れない	nemure nai
sleeping pill	睡眠薬	suiminyaku
to take a sleeping pill	睡眠薬を服用する	suiminyaku wo fukuyō suru
to feel sleepy	眠気を催す	nemuke wo moyōsu
to yawn (vi)	あくびをする	akubi wo suru
to go to bed	就寝する	shūshin suru
to make up the bed	ベッドを整える	beddo wo totonoeru
to fall asleep	寝入る	neiru
nightmare	悪夢	akumu
snoring	いびき［鼾］	ibiki
to snore (vi)	いびきをかく	ibiki wo kaku
alarm clock	目覚まし時計	mezamashi dokei
to wake (vt)	起こす	okosu
to wake up	起きる	okiru
to get up (vi)	起床する	kishō suru
to wash up (vi)	洗面する	senmen suru

61.

62.

answer	回答	kaitō
truth	真実	shinjitsu
lie	うそ［嘘］	uso
thought	思索	shisaku
idea (inspiration)	考え	kangae
fantasy	空想	kūsō

63.

to demand (request firmly)	要求する	yōkyū suru
to tease (nickname)	からかう	karakau
to mock (make fun of)	あざ笑う	azawarau
mockery, derision	あざ笑い	azawarai
nickname	あだ名	adana
allusion	ほのめかし	honomekashi
to allude (vi)	ほのめかす	honomekasu
to imply (vt)	意味する	imi suru
description	記述すること	kijutsu suru koto
to describe (vt)	記述する	kijutsu suru
praise (compliments)	称賛	shōsan
to praise (vt)	称賛する	shōsan suru
disappointment	失望	shitsubō
to disappoint (vt)	失望させる	shitsubō saseru
to be disappointed	失望する	shitsubō suru
supposition	仮定	katei
to suppose (assume)	仮定する	katei suru
warning (caution)	警告	keikoku
to warn (vt)	警告する	keikoku suru

64.

sigh	ため息 [ためいき]	tameiki
to sigh (vi)	ため息をつく	tameiki wo tsuku
to shudder (vi)	身震いする	miburui suru
gesture	身ぶり	miburi
to touch (one's arm, etc.)	触れる	fureru
to seize (by the arm)	握る	nigiru
to tap (on the shoulder)	軽くたたく	karuku tataku
Look out!	危ない！	abunai!
Really?	本当ですか？	hontō desu ka ?
Are you sure?	本当に？	hontōni ?
Good luck!	幸運を！	kōun o!
I see!	分かった！	wakatta!
It's a pity!	残念！	zannen!

65.

66.

complaint	不平	fuhei
to complain (vi, vt)	不平を言う	fuhei wo iu
apology	謝罪	shazai
to apologize (vi)	謝罪する	shazai suru
to beg pardon	謝る	ayamaru
criticism	批判	hihan
to criticize (vt)	批判する	hihan suru
accusation	責め	seme
to accuse (vt)	責める	semeru
revenge	復讐	fukushū
to revenge (vt)	復讐する	fukushū suru
to pay back	仕返しをする	shikaeshi wo suru
disdain	軽蔑	keibetsu
to despise (vt)	軽蔑する	keibetsu suru
hatred, hate	憎しみ	nikushimi
to hate (vt)	憎む	nikumu
nervous (adj)	緊張した	kinchō shita
to be nervous	緊張する	kinchō suru
angry (mad)	怒って	okotte
to make angry	怒らせる	okoraseru
humiliation	屈辱	kutsujoku
to humiliate (vt)	屈辱を与える	kutsujoku wo ataeru
to humiliate oneself	面目を失う	menboku wo ushinau
shock	衝撃	shōgeki
to shock (vt)	衝撃を与える	shōgeki wo ataeru
trouble (annoyance)	不愉快なこと	fuyukai na koto
unpleasant (adj)	不愉快な	fuyukai na
fear (dread)	恐れ	osore
terrible (storm, heat)	ひどい	hidoi
scary (e.g., ~ story)	怖い	kowai
horror	恐怖	kyōfu
awful (crime, news)	恐ろしい	osoroshī
to begin to tremble	震え始める	furue hajimeru
to cry (weep)	泣く	naku
to start crying	泣きだす	nakidasu
tear	涙	namida
fault	責任	sekinin
guilt (feeling)	罪悪感	zaiaku kan
dishonor (disgrace)	不名誉	fumeiyo
protest	抗議	kōgi
stress	ストレス	sutoresu

to disturb (vt)	邪魔をする	jama wo suru
to be furious	腹を立てる	hara wo tateru
mad, angry (adj)	腹を立てた	hara wo tate ta
to end (~ a relationship)	終わらせる	owaraseru
to swear (at sb)	しかる	shikaru
to be scared	恐れる	osoreru
to hit (strike with hand)	ぶつ	butsu
to fight (vi)	喧嘩をする	kenka wo suru
to settle (a conflict)	解決する	kaiketsu suru
discontented (adj)	不満な	fuman na
furious (adj)	激怒した	gekido shi ta
It's not good!	良くないよ！	yoku nai yo!
It's bad!	いけないことだぞ！	ike nai koto da zo!

atherosclerosis	アテローム性動脈硬化	ate rōmu sei dōmyaku kōka
gastritis	胃炎	ien
appendicitis	虫垂炎	chūsuien
cholecystitis	胆嚢炎	tannō en
ulcer	潰瘍	kaiyō
measles	麻疹	hashika
German measles	風疹	fūshin
jaundice	黄疸	ōdan
hepatitis	肝炎	kanen
schizophrenia	統合失調症	tōgō shicchō shō
rabies (hydrophobia)	恐水病	kyōsuibyō
neurosis	神経症	shinkeishō
concussion	脳震とう（脳震盪）	nōshintō
cancer	がん［癌］	gan
sclerosis	硬化症	kōka shō
multiple sclerosis	多発性硬化症	tahatsu sei kōka shō
alcoholism	アルコール依存症	arukōru izon shō
alcoholic (n)	アルコール依存症患者	arukōru izon shō kanja
syphilis	梅毒	baidoku
AIDS	エイズ	eizu
tumor	腫瘍	shuyō
malignant (adj)	悪性の	akusei no
benign (adj)	良性の	ryōsei no
fever	発熱	hatsunetsu
malaria	マラリア	mararia
gangrene	壊疽	eso
seasickness	船酔い	fune yoi
epilepsy	てんかん［癲癇］	tenkan
epidemic	伝染病	densen byō
typhus	チフス	chifusu
tuberculosis	結核	kekkaku
cholera	コレラ	korera
plague (bubonic ~)	ペスト	pesuto

69.

shivering	震え	furue
pale (e.g., ~ face)	青白い	aojiroi
cough	咳	seki
to cough (vi)	咳をする	seki wo suru
to sneeze (vi)	くしゃみをする	kushami wo suru
faint	気絶	kizetsu
to faint (vi)	気絶する	kizetsu suru
bruise (hématome)	打ち身	uchimi
bump (lump)	たんこぶ	tankobu
to bruise oneself	あざができる	aza ga dekiru
bruise (contusion)	打撲傷	dabokushō
to get bruised	打撲する	daboku suru
to limp (vi)	足を引きずる	ashi wo hikizuru
dislocation	脱臼	dakkyū
to dislocate (vt)	脱臼する	dakkyū suru
fracture	骨折	kossetsu
to have a fracture	骨折する	kossetsu suru
cut (e.g., paper ~)	切り傷	kirikizu
to cut oneself	切り傷を負う	kirikizu wo ō
bleeding	出血	shukketsu
burn (injury)	火傷	yakedo
to scald oneself	火傷する	yakedo suru
to prick (vt)	刺す	sasu
to prick oneself	自分を刺す	jibun wo sasu
to injure (vt)	けがする	kega suru
injury	けが［怪我］	kega
wound	負傷	fushō
trauma	外傷	gaishō
to be delirious	熱に浮かされる	netsu ni ukasareru
to stutter (vi)	どもる	domoru
sunstroke	日射病	nisshabyō

70.

delivery, labor	分娩	bumben
to deliver (~ a baby)	分娩する	bumben suru
abortion	妊娠中絶	ninshin chūzetsu
breathing, respiration	呼吸	kokyū
inhalation	息を吸うこと	iki wo sū koto
exhalation	息を吐くこと	iki wo haku koto
to exhale (vi)	息を吐く	iki wo haku
to inhale (vi)	息を吸う	iki wo sū
disabled person	障害者	shōgai sha
cripple	身障者	shinshōsha
drug addict	麻薬中毒者	mayaku chūdoku sha
deaf (adj)	ろうの［聾の］	rō no
dumb, mute	口のきけない	kuchi no kike nai
deaf-and-dumb (adj)	ろうあの［聾唖の］	rōa no
mad, insane (adj)	狂気の	kyōki no
madman	狂人	kyōjin
madwoman	狂女	kyōjo
to go insane	気が狂う	ki ga kurū
gene	遺伝子	idenshi
immunity	免疫	meneki
hereditary (adj)	遺伝性の	iden sei no
congenital (adj)	先天性の	senten sei no
virus	ウィルス	wirusu
microbe	細菌	saikin
bacterium	バクテリア	bakuteria
infection	伝染	densen

71.

to vaccinate (vt)	予防接種をする	yobō sesshu wo suru
injection, shot	注射	chūsha
to give an injection	注射する	chūsha suru
attack	発作	hossa
amputation	切断手術	setsudan shujutsu
to amputate (vt)	切断する	setsudan suru
coma	昏睡	konsui
to be in a coma	昏睡状態になる	konsui jōtai ni naru
intensive care	集中治療	shūchū chiryō
to recover (~ from flu)	回復する	kaifuku suru
state (patient's ~)	体調	taichō
consciousness	意識	ishiki
memory (faculty)	記憶	kioku
to extract (tooth)	抜く	nuku
filling	詰め物	tsume mono
to fill (a tooth)	詰め物をする	tsume mono wo suru
hypnosis	催眠術	saimin jutsu
to hypnotize (vt)	催眠術をかける	saimin jutsu wo kakeru

72.

ampule	アンプル	anpuru
mixture	調合薬	chōgō yaku
syrup	シロップ	shiroppu
pill	丸剤	gan zai
powder	粉薬	konagusuri
bandage	包帯	hōtai
cotton wool	脱脂綿	dasshimen
iodine	ヨード	yōdo
Band-Aid	ばんそうこう［絆創膏］	bansōkō
eyedropper	アイドロッパー	aidoroppā
thermometer	体温計	taionkei
syringe	注射器	chūsha ki
wheelchair	車椅子	kurumaisu
crutches	松葉杖	matsubazue
painkiller	痛み止め	itami tome
laxative	下剤	gezai
spirit (ethanol)	エタノール	etanoru
medicinal herbs	薬草	yakusō
herbal (~ tea)	薬草の	yakusō no

74.

skyscraper	摩天楼	matenrō
facade	ファサード	fasādo
roof	屋根	yane
window	窓	mado
arch	アーチ	āchi
column	柱	hashira
corner	角	kado
store window	ショーウインドー	shōuindō
store sign	店看板	mise kanban
poster	ポスター	posutā
advertising poster	広告ポスター	kōkoku posutā
billboard	広告掲示板	kōkoku keijiban
garbage, trash	ゴミ [ごみ]	gomi
garbage can	ゴミ入れ	gomi ire
to litter (vi)	ゴミを投げ捨てる	gomi wo nagesuteru
garbage dump	ゴミ捨て場	gomi suteba
phone booth	電話ボックス	denwa bokkusu
lamppost	街灯柱	gaitō bashira
bench (park ~)	ベンチ	benchi
police officer	警官	keikan
police	警察	keisatsu
beggar	こじき	kojiki
homeless, bum	ホームレス	hōmuresu

76.

post office	郵便局	yūbin kyoku
dry cleaners	クリーニング屋	kurīningu ya
photo studio	写真館	shashin kan
shoe store	靴屋	kutsuya
bookstore	本屋	honya
sporting goods store	スポーツ店	supōtsu ten
clothes repair	洋服直し専門店	yōfuku naoshi senmon ten
formal wear rental	貸衣裳店	kashi ishō ten
movie rental store	レンタルビデオ店	rentarubideo ten
circus	サーカス	sākasu
zoo	動物園	dōbutsu en
movie theater	映画館	eiga kan
museum	博物館	hakubutsukan
library	図書館	toshokan
theater	劇場	gekijō
opera	オペラハウス	opera hausu
nightclub	ナイトクラブ	naito kurabu
casino	カジノ	kajino
mosque	モスク	mosuku
synagogue	シナゴーグ	shinagōgu
cathedral	大聖堂	dai seidō
temple	寺院	jīn
church	教会	kyōkai
college	大学	daigaku
university	大学	daigaku
school	学校	gakkō
prefecture	県庁舎	ken chōsha
city hall	市役所	shiyaku sho
hotel	ホテル	hoteru
bank	銀行	ginkō
embassy	大使館	taishikan
travel agency	旅行代理店	ryokō dairi ten
information office	案内所	annai sho
money exchange	両替所	ryōgae sho
subway	地下鉄	chikatetsu
hospital	病院	byōin
gas station	ガソリンスタンド	gasorin sutando
parking lot	駐車場	chūsha jō

77.

78.

check out, cash desk	レジ	reji
mirror	鏡	kagami
counter (in shop)	カウンター	kauntā
fitting room	試着室	shichaku shitsu
to try on	試着する	shichaku suru
to fit (ab. dress, etc.)	合う	au
to like (I like ...)	好む	konomu
price	価格	kakaku
price tag	値札	nefuda
to cost (vt)	かかる	kakaru
How much?	いくら？	ikura ?
discount	割引	waribiki
inexpensive (adj)	安価な	anka na
cheap (adj)	安い	yasui
expensive (adj)	高い	takai
It's expensive	それは高い	sore wa takai
rental (n)	レンタル	rentaru
to rent (~ a tuxedo)	レンタルする	rentaru suru
credit	信用取引	shinyō torihiki
on credit (adv)	付けで	tsuke de

80.

to deposit into the account	口座に預金する	kōza ni yokin suru
to withdraw (vt)	引き出す	hikidasu
credit card	クレジットカード	kurejitto kādo
cash	現金	genkin
check	小切手	kogitte
to write a check	小切手を書く	kogitte wo kaku
checkbook	小切手帳	kogitte chō
wallet	財布	saifu
change purse	小銭入れ	kozeni ire
billfold	札入れ	satsu ire
safe	金庫	kinko
heir	相続人	sōzokunin
inheritance	相続	sōzoku
fortune (wealth)	財産	zaisan
lease, rent	賃貸	chintai
rent money	家賃	yachin
to rent (sth from sb)	借りる	kariru
price	価格	kakaku
cost	費用	hiyō
sum	合計金額	gōkei kingaku
to spend (vt)	お金を使う	okane wo tsukau
expenses	出費	shuppi
to economize (vi, vt)	倹約する	kenyaku suru
economical	節約の	setsuyaku no
to pay (vi, vt)	払う	harau
payment	支払い	shiharai
change (give the ~)	おつり	o tsuri
tax	税	zei
fine	罰金	bakkin
to fine (vt)	罰金を科す	bakkin wo kasu

81.

parcel	小包	kozutsumi
money transfer	送金	sōkin
to receive (vt)	受け取る	uketoru
to send (vt)	送る	okuru
sending	送信	sōshin
address	住所	jūsho
ZIP code	郵便番号	yūbin bangō
sender	送り主	okurinushi
receiver, addressee	受取人	uketorinin
name	名前	namae
family name	姓	sei
rate (of postage)	郵便料金	yūbin ryōkin
standard (adj)	通常の	tsūjō no
economical (adj)	エコノミー航空	ekonomīkōkū
weight	重さ	omo sa
to weigh up (vt)	量る	hakaru
envelope	封筒	fūtō
postage stamp	郵便切手	yūbin kitte
to stamp an envelope	封筒に切手を貼る	fūtō ni kitte wo haru

to come down	下りる	oriru
to move (to new premises)	移転する	iten suru

83.

ringing (sound)	音	oto
doorbell	ドアベル	doa beru
doorbell button	玄関ブザー	genkan buzā
knock (at the door)	ノック	nokku
to knock (vi)	ノックする	nokku suru
code	コード	kōdo
code lock	ダイヤル錠	daiyaru jō
door phone	インターホン	intāhon
number (on the door)	番号	bangō
doorplate	表札	hyōsatsu
peephole	ドアアイ	doaai

85.

moat	堀	hori
chain	鎖	kusari
arrow loop	矢狭間	ya hazama
magnificent (adj)	華麗な	karei na
majestic (adj)	壮大な	sōdai na
impregnable (adj)	難攻不落の	nankōfuraku no
medieval (adj)	中世の	chūsei no

87.

89.

91.

bottle	ボトル	botoru
jar (glass)	ジャー、瓶	jā, bin
can	缶	kan
bottle opener	栓抜き	sen nuki
can opener	缶切り	kankiri
corkscrew	コルク抜き	koruku nuki
filter	フィルター	firutā
to filter (vt)	フィルターにかける	firutā ni kakeru
trash	ゴミ［ごみ］	gomi
trash can	ゴミ箱	gomibako

92.

93.

wallpaper	壁紙	kabegami
to wallpaper (vt)	壁紙を貼る	kabegami wo haru
varnish	ニス	nisu
to varnish (vt)	ニスを塗る	nisu wo nuru

95.

dangerous (adj)	危険な	kiken na
to catch fire	火がつく	higatsuku
explosion	爆発	bakuhatsu
to set fire	放火する	hōka suru
incendiary (arsonist)	放火犯人	hōka hannin
arson	放火	hōka
to blaze (vi)	燃え盛る	moesakaru
to burn (be on fire)	燃える	moeru
to burn down	焼き尽くす	yakitsukusu
to call the fire department	消防署に電話する	shōbōsho ni denwasuru
fireman	消防士	shōbō shi
fire truck	消防車	shōbōsha
fire department	消防署	shōbō sho
fire truck ladder	屈折はしご	kussetsu hashigo
fire hose	消防用ホース	shōbō yō hōsu
fire extinguisher	消火器	shōka ki
helmet	ヘルメット	herumetto
siren	サイレン	sairen
to call out	叫ぶ	sakebu
to call for help	助けを求める	tasuke wo motomeru
rescuer	救助員	kyūjo in
to rescue (vt)	救助する	kyūjo suru
to arrive (vi)	到着する	tōchaku suru
to extinguish (vt)	火を消す	hi wo kesu
water	水	mizu
sand	砂	suna
ruins (destruction)	焼け跡	yakeato
to collapse (building, etc.)	崩壊する	hōkai suru
to fall down (vi)	崩れ落ちる	kuzureochiru
to cave in (ceiling, floor)	崩れる	kuzureru
piece of wreckage	残骸の破片	zangai no hahen
ash	灰	hai
to suffocate (die)	窒息死する	chissokushi suru
to be killed (perish)	枯れる	kareru

to give a loan	融資を行う	yūshi wo okonau
guarantee	保障	hoshō

98.

menu	メニュー	menyū
settings	設定	settei
tune (melody)	メロディー	merodī
to select (vt)	選択する	sentaku suru
calculator	電卓	dentaku
voice mail	ボイスメール	boisu mēru
alarm clock	目覚まし	mezamashi
contacts	連絡先	renraku saki
SMS (text message)	テキストメッセージ	tekisuto messēji
subscriber	加入者	kanyū sha

100.

great (~ scandal)	大きな	ōkina
program	番組	bangumi
interview	インタビュー	intabyū
live broadcast	生放送	namahōsō
channel	チャンネル	channeru

102.

to pasture (vt)	放牧する	hōboku suru
herdsman	牧夫	bokufu
pastureland	牧草地	bokusō chi
cattle breeding	牧畜	bokuchiku
sheep farming	牧羊	bokuyō
plantation	プランテーション	purantēshon
row (garden bed ~s)	畝	une
hothouse	ビニールハウス	binīru hausu
drought (lack of rain)	干ばつ	kanbatsu
dry (~ summer)	干ばつの	kanbatsu no
grain	穀物	kokumotsu
cereal crops	禾穀類	kakokurui
to harvest, to gather	収穫する	shūkaku suru
miller (person)	製粉業者	seifun gyōsha
mill (e.g., gristmill)	製粉所	seifun sho
to grind (grain)	挽く	hiku
flour	小麦粉	komugiko
straw	わら［藁］	wara

103.

to plaster (vt)	しっくいを塗る	shikkui wo nuru
paint	塗料	toryō
to paint (~ a wall)	塗る	nuru
barrel	樽	taru
crane	クレーン、起重機	kurēn, kijūki
to lift (vt)	上げる	ageru
to lower (vt)	下げる	sageru
bulldozer	ブルドーザー	burudōzā
excavator	バックホー	bakkuhō
scoop, bucket	バケット	baketto
to dig (excavate)	掘る	horu
hard hat	安全ヘルメット	anzen herumetto

chairman	会長	kaichō
deputy (substitute)	副部長	fuku buchō
assistant	助手	joshu
secretary	秘書	hisho
personal assistant	個人秘書	kojin hisho
businessman	ビジネスマン	bijinesuman
entrepreneur	企業家	kigyō ka
founder	創立者	sōritsu sha
to found (vt)	創立する	sōritsu suru
incorporator	共同出資者	kyōdō shusshi sha
partner	パートナー	pātonā
stockholder	株主	kabunushi
millionaire	百万長者	hyakuman chōja
billionaire	億万長者	okuman chōja
owner, proprietor	経営者	keieisha
landowner	土地所有者	tochi shoyū sha
client	クライアント	kuraianto
regular client	常連客	jōren kyaku
buyer (customer)	買い手	kaite
visitor	来客	raikyaku
professional (n)	熟練者	jukuren sha
expert	エキスパート	ekisupāto
specialist	専門家	senmon ka
banker	銀行家	ginkō ka
broker	仲買人	nakagainin
cashier, teller	レジ係	reji gakari
accountant	会計士	kaikeishi
security guard	警備員	keibi in
investor	投資者	tōshi sha
debtor	債務者	saimu sha
creditor	債権者	saiken sha
borrower	借り主	karinushi
importer	輸入業者	yunyū gyōsha
exporter	輸出業者	yushutsu gyōsha
manufacturer	メーカー	mēkā
distributor	代理店	dairi ten
middleman	中間業者	chūkan gyōsha
consultant	コンサルタント	konsarutanto
sales representative	販売外交員	hanbai gaikōin
agent	代理人	dairinin
insurance agent	保険代理人	hoken dairinin

106.

lieutenant	中尉	chūi
captain	大尉	taī
major	少佐	shōsa
colonel	大佐	taisa
general	将官	shōkan
marshal	元帥	gensui
admiral	提督	teitoku
military man	軍人	gunjin
soldier	兵士	heishi
officer	士官	shikan
commander	指揮官	shiki kan
border guard	国境警備兵	kokkyō keibi hei
radio operator	通信士	tsūshin shi
scout (searcher)	斥候	sekkō
pioneer (sapper)	工兵	kōhei
marksman	射手	shashu
navigator	航空士	kōkū shi

108.

monk	修道士	shūdō shi
abbot	修道院長	shūdōin chō
rabbi	ラビ	rabi
vizier	ワズィール	wazīru
shah	シャー	shā
sheikh	シャイフ	shaifu

109.

poet	詩人	shijin
sculptor	彫刻家	chōkoku ka
artist (painter)	画家	gaka
juggler	手品師	tejina shi
clown	道化師	dōkeshi
acrobat	曲芸師	kyokugei shi
magician	手品師	tejina shi

111.

typist (fem.)	タイピスト	taipisuto
designer	デザイナー	dezainā
computer expert	コンピュータ専門家	konpyūta senmon ka
programmer	プログラマー	puroguramā
engineer (designer)	技師	gishi
sailor	水夫	suifu
seaman	船員	senin
rescuer	救助員	kyūjo in
fireman	消防士	shōbō shi
policeman	警官	keikan
watchman	警備員	keibi in
detective	探偵	tantei
customs officer	税関吏	zeikanri
bodyguard	ボディーガード	bodīgādo
prison guard	刑務官	keimu kan
inspector	検査官	kensakan
sportsman	スポーツマン	supōtsuman
trainer, coach	トレーナー	torēnā
butcher	肉屋	nikuya
cobbler	靴修理屋	kutsu shūri ya
merchant	商人	shōnin
loader (person)	荷役作業員	niyakusa gyōin
fashion designer	ファッションデザイナー	fasshon dezainā
model (fem.)	モデル	moderu

112.

hippie	ヒッピー	hippī
bandit	山賊	sanzoku
hit man, killer	殺し屋	koroshi ya
drug addict	麻薬中毒者	mayaku chūdoku sha
drug dealer	麻薬の売人	mayaku no bainin
prostitute (fem.)	売春婦	baishun fu
pimp	ポン引き	pon biki
sorcerer	魔法使い	mahōtsukai
sorceress	女魔法使い	jo mahōtsukai
pirate	海賊	kaizoku
slave	奴隷	dorei
samurai	侍、武士	samurai, bushi
savage (primitive)	未開人	mikai jin

alpinism	登山	tozan
alpinist	登山家	tozan ka
running	ランニング	ranningu
runner	ランナー	rannā
athletics	陸上競技	rikujō kyōgi
athlete	陸上競技者	rikujō kyōgi sha
horseback riding	乗馬	jōba
horse rider	乗馬者	jōba sha
figure skating	フィギュアスケート	figyua sukēto
figure skater (masc.)	フィギュアスケート選手	figyua sukēto senshu
figure skater (fem.)	フィギュアスケート選手	figyua sukēto senshu
weightlifting	重量挙げ	jūryōage
weightlifter	重量挙げ選手	jūryōage senshu
car racing	カーレース	kā rēsu
racing driver	カーレーサー	kā rēsā
cycling	サイクリング	saikuringu
cyclist	サイクリスト	saikurisuto
broad jump	幅跳び	habatobi
pole vault	棒高跳び	bōtakatobi
jumper	跳躍選手	chōyaku senshu

114.

snowboarding	スノーボート	sunōbōto
archery	洋弓	yōkyū

115.

stadium	スタジアム	sutajiamu
stand (bleachers)	観覧席	kanranseki
fan, supporter	ファン	fan
opponent, rival	競争相手	kyōsō aite
start	スタート	sutāto
finish line	ゴール	gōru
defeat	負け	make
to lose (not win)	負ける	makeru
referee	レフェリー	referī
jury	審判団	shinpan dan
score	スコア	sukoa
draw	引き分け	hikiwake
to draw (vi)	引き分けになる	hikiwake ni naru
point	点	ten
result (final score)	得点	tokuten
period	ピリオド	piriodo
half-time	ハーフタイム	hāfu taimu
doping	ドーピング	dōpingu
to penalize (vt)	ペナルティーを与える	penarutī wo ataeru
to disqualify (vt)	失格にする	shikkaku ni suru
apparatus	器具	kigu
javelin	やり［槍］	yari
shot put ball	砲丸	hōgan
ball (snooker, etc.)	ボール	bōru
aim (target)	的	mato
target	標的	hyōteki
to shoot (vi)	撃つ	utsu
precise (~ shot)	正確な	seikaku na
trainer, coach	トレーナー	torēnā
to train (sb)	トレーニングする	torēningu suru
to train (vi)	トレーニングする	torēningu suru
training	トレーニング	torēningu
gym	体育館	taīkukan
exercise (physical)	運動	undō
warm-up (of athlete)	ウォーミングアップ	wōminguappu

to punish (vt)	罰する	bassuru
punishment	罰	batsu
conduct (behavior)	行動	kōdō
report card	通信簿	tsūshin bo
pencil	鉛筆	enpitsu
eraser	消しゴム	keshigomu
chalk	チョーク	chōku
pencil case	筆箱	fudebako
schoolbag	通学カバン	tsūgaku kaban
pen	ペン	pen
school notebook	ノート	nōto
textbook	教科書	kyōkasho
compasses	コンパス	konpasu
to draw (a blueprint, etc.)	製図する	seizu suru
technical drawing	製図	seizu
poem	詩	shi
by heart (adv)	暗記して	anki shi te
to learn by heart	暗記する	anki suru
school vacation	休暇	kyūka
to be on vacation	休暇中である	kyūka chū de aru
to spend one's vacation	休暇を過ごす	kyūka wo sugosu
test (written math ~)	筆記試験	hikki shiken
essay (composition)	論文式試験	ronbun shiki shiken
dictation	書き取り	kakitori
exam	試験	shiken
to take an exam	試験を受ける	shiken wo ukeru
experiment (chemical ~)	実験	jikken

118.

lecture	講義	kōgi
course mate	同級生	dōkyūsei
scholarship	奨学金	shōgaku kin
academic degree	学位	gakui

119.

apostrophe	アポストロフィー	aposutorofī
period, dot	句点	kuten
comma	コンマ	konma
semicolon	セミコロン	semikoron
colon	コロン	koron
ellipsis	省略	shōrya ku
question mark	疑問符	gimon fu
exclamation point	感嘆符	kantan fu
quotation marks	引用符	inyō fu
in quotation marks	引用符内	inyō fu nai
parenthesis	ガッコ（括弧）	gakko
in parenthesis	ガッコ内 （括弧内）	kakko nai
hyphen	ハイフン	haifun
dash	ダッシュ	dasshu
space (between words)	スペース	supēsu
letter	文字	moji
capital letter	大文字	daimonji
vowel (n)	母音	boin
consonant (n)	子音	shīn
sentence	文	bun
subject	主語	shugo
predicate	述語	jutsugo
line	行	gyō
on a new line	新しい行で	atarashī gyō de
paragraph	段落	danraku
word	単語	tango
group of words	語群	gogun
expression	表現	hyōgen
synonym	同義語	dōgigo
antonym	対義語	taigigo
rule	規則	kisoku
exception	例外	reigai
correct (adj)	正しい	tadashī
conjugation	活用	katsuyō
declension	語形変化	gokei henka
nominal case	名詞格	meishi kaku
question	疑問文	gimon bun
to underline (vt)	下線を引く	kasen wo hiku
dotted line	点線	tensen

121.

polyglot	ポリグロット	porigurotto
memory	記憶	kioku

122.

scene (e.g., the last ~)	場	ba
act	幕	maku
intermission	幕間	makuai

125.

movie set	映画のセット	eiga no setto
camera	カメラ	kamera
movie theater	映画館	eiga kan
screen (e.g., big ~)	スクリーン	sukurīn
to show a movie	映画を上映する	eiga wo jōei suru
soundtrack	サウンドトラック	saundotorakku
special effects	特撮	tokusatsu
subtitles	字幕	jimaku
credits	クレジット	kurejitto
translation	訳	yaku

126.

sketch	スケッチ	sukecchi
paint	絵具	enogu
watercolor	水彩絵具	suisai enogu
oil (paint)	油絵具	abura enogu
pencil	鉛筆	enpitsu
Indian ink	墨	sumi
charcoal	木炭	mokutan
to draw (vi, vt)	描く	egaku
to paint (vi, vt)	絵の具で描く	enogu de egaku
to pose (vi)	ポーズを取る	pōzu wo toru
artist's model (masc.)	ヌードモデル	nūdo moderu
artist's model (fem.)	ヌードモデル	nūdo moderu
artist (painter)	画家	gaka
work of art	美術品	bijutsu hin
masterpiece	傑作	kessaku
artist's workshop	画家のアトリエ	gaka no atorie
canvas (cloth)	画布	gafu
easel	イーゼル	īzeru
palette	パレット	paretto
frame (of picture, etc.)	額縁	gakubuchi
restoration	修復	shūfuku
to restore (vt)	修復する	shūfuku suru

127.

poem (epic, ballad)	叙事詩	jojishi
poet	詩人	shijin
fiction	フィクション	fikushon
science fiction	サイエンスフィクション	saiensu fikushon
adventures	冒険	bōken
educational literature	教材	kyōzai
children's literature	児童文学	jidō bungaku

128.

musical instrument	楽器	gakki
to play ...	演奏する	ensō suru
guitar	ギター	gitā
violin	バイオリン	baiorin
cello	チェロ	chero
double bass	コントラバス	kontorabasu
harp	ハープ	hāpu
piano	ピアノ	piano
grand piano	グランドピアノ	gurando piano
organ	オルガン	orugan
wind instruments	管楽器	kangakki
oboe	オーボエ	ōboe
saxophone	サクソフォーン	sakusofōn
clarinet	クラリネット	kurarinetto
flute	フルート	furūto
trumpet	トランペット	toranpetto
accordion	アコーディオン	akōdion
drum	ドラム	doramu
duo	二重奏	nijūsō
trio	三重奏	sanjūsō
quartet	四重奏	shijūsō
choir	合唱団	gasshō dan
orchestra	管弦楽団	kangengaku dan
pop music	ポップミュージック	poppu myūjikku
rock music	ロックミュージック	rokku myūjikku
rock group	ロックバンド	rokku bando
jazz	ジャズ	jazu
idol	アイドル	aidoru
admirer, fan	ファン	fan
concert	コンサート	konsāto
symphony	交響曲	kōkyō kyoku
composition	作曲	sakkyoku
to compose (write)	書く	kaku
singing	歌うこと	utau koto
song	歌	uta
tune (melody)	メロディー	merodī
rhythm	リズム	rizumu
blues	ブルース	burūsu
sheet music	楽譜	gakufu
baton	指揮棒	shikibō
bow	弓	yumi
string	げん	gen
case (e.g., guitar ~)	ケース	kēsu

131.

reading (activity)	読書	dokusho
silently (to oneself)	黙って	damatte
aloud (adv)	声に出して	koe ni dashi te
to publish (vt)	出版する	shuppan suru
publishing (process)	出版業	shuppan gyō
publisher	発行者	hakkō sha
publishing house	出版社	shuppan sha
to come out (be released)	出版される	shuppan sareru
release (of a book)	発売、公開	hatsubai, kōkai
print run	発行部数	hakkō busū
bookstore	本屋	honya
library	図書館	toshokan
story (novella)	中編小説	chūhen shōsetsu
short story	短編小説	tanpen shōsetsu
novel	小説	shōsetsu
detective novel	探偵小説	tantei shōsetsu
memoirs	回想録	kaisō roku
legend	伝説	densetsu
myth	神話	shinwa
poetry, poems	詩	shi
autobiography	自伝	jiden
selected works	選集	senshū
science fiction	サイエンスフィクション	saiensu fikushon
title	題名	daimei
introduction	前書き	maegaki
title page	表題紙	hyōdai shi
chapter	章	shō
extract	抜粋	bassui
episode	挿話	sōwa
plot (storyline)	筋	suji
contents	目次	mokuji
table of contents	目次	mokuji
main character	主人公	shujinkō
volume	巻	kan
cover	表紙	hyōshi
binding	装丁	sōtei
bookmark	しおり	shiori
page	頁	pēji
to flick through	パラパラとめくる	parapara to mekuru
margins	余白	yohaku
annotation	注釈	chūshaku

footnote	脚注	kyakuchū
text	文章	bunshō
type, font	フォント	fonto
misprint, typo	タイプミス	taipu misu
translation	翻訳	honyaku
to translate (vt)	翻訳する	honyaku suru
original (n)	原作	gensaku
famous (adj)	有名な	yūmei na
unknown (adj)	無名の	mumei no
interesting (adj)	面白い	omoshiroi
bestseller	ベストセラー	besutoserā
dictionary	辞書	jisho
textbook	教科書	kyōkasho
encyclopedia	百科事典	hyakka jiten

133.

to bite (ab. fish)	食いつく	kuitsuku
catch (of fish)	釣果	chōka
ice-hole	氷の穴	kōri no ana
fishing net	漁網	gyomō
boat	ボート	bōto
to net (catch with net)	網で捕らえる	ami de toraeru
to cast the net	投網を打つ	nageami wo utsu
to haul in the net	網を手繰り寄せる	ami wo taguriyoseru
to fall into the net	網にかかる	ami ni kakaru
whaler (person)	捕鯨者	hogei sha
whaleboat	捕鯨船	hogei sen
harpoon	銛	mori

134.

136.

exposure time	露光時間	rokō jikan
viewfinder	ファインダー	faindā
digital camera	デジタルカメラ	dejitaru kamera
tripod	三脚	sankyaku
flash	フラッシュ	furasshu
to photograph (vt)	撮影する	satsuei suru
to take pictures	写真をとる	shashin wo toru
to be photographed	写真を撮られる	shashin wo torareru
focus	ピント	pinto
to adjust the focus	ピントを調整する	pinto wo chōsei suru
sharp, in focus (adj)	シャープ	shāpu
sharpness	シャープネス	shāpu nesu
contrast	コントラスト	kontorasuto
contrasty (adj)	コントラストの	kontorasuto no
picture (photo)	写真	shashin
negative (n)	ネガ	nega
film (a roll of ~)	写真フィルム	shashin firumu
frame (still)	コマ	koma
to print (photos)	印刷する	insatsu suru

138.

surfing	サーフィン	sāfin
surfer	サーファー	sāfā
scuba set	スキューバダイビング用品	sukyūba daibingu yōhin
flippers (swimfins)	フィン	fin
mask	マスク	masuku
diver	ダイバー	daibā
to dive (vi)	ダイビングする	daibingu suru
underwater (adv)	水中に	suichū ni
beach umbrella	ビーチパラソル	bīchi parasoru
beach chair	ビーチチェア	bīchi chea
sunglasses	サングラス	sangurasu
air mattress	エアーマットレス	eā mattoresu
to play (amuse oneself)	遊ぶ	asobu
to go for a swim	海水浴をする	kaisuiyoku wo suru
beach ball	ビーチボール	bīchi bōru
to inflate (vt)	膨らませる	fukuramaseru
inflatable, air- (adj)	エア…	ea …
wave	波	nami
buoy	ブイ	bui
to drown (ab. person)	溺れる	oboreru
to save, to rescue	救出する	kyūshutsu suru
life vest	ライフジャケット	raifu jaketto
to observe, to watch	監視する	kanshi suru
lifeguard	監視員	kanshi in

password	パスワード	pasuwādo
virus	ウイルス	uirusu
to find, to detect	検出する	kenshutsu suru
byte	バイト	baito
megabyte	メガバイト	megabaito
data	データ	dēta
database	データベース	dētabēsu
cable (USB, etc.)	ケーブル	kēburu
to disconnect (vt)	接続を切る	setsuzoku wo kiru
to connect (sth to sth)	接続する	setsuzoku suru

140.

connection (ADSL, etc.)	接続	setsuzoku
speed	速度	sokudo
modem	モデム	modemu
access	アクセス	akusesu
port (e.g., input ~)	ポート	pōto
connection (make a ~)	接続	setsuzoku
to connect to ... (vi)	…に接続する	... ni setsuzoku suru
to select (vt)	選択する	sentaku suru
to search (for ...)	検索する	kensaku suru

airplane window	機窓	kisō
aisle	通路	tsūro

142.

train wreck	鉄道事故	tetsudō jiko
to be derailed	脱線する	dassen suru
steam engine	蒸気機関車	jōki kikan sha
stoker, fireman	火夫	kafu
firebox	火室	kashitsu
coal	石炭	sekitan

143.

screw propeller プロペラ puropera
cabin 船室 senshitsu
wardroom 士官室 shikan shitsu
engine room 機関室 kikan shitsu
bridge 船橋 funabashi
radio room 無線室 musen shitsu
wave (radio) 電波 denpa
logbook 航海日誌 kōkai nisshi

spyglass 単眼望遠鏡 tangan bōenkyō
bell 船鐘 funekane
flag 旗 hata

rope (mooring ~) ロープ rōpu
knot (bowline, etc.) 結び目 musubime
deckrail 手摺 tesuri
gangway 舷門 genmon

anchor 錨［いかり］ ikari
to weigh anchor 錨をあげる ikari wo ageru
to drop anchor 錨を下ろす ikari wo orosu
anchor chain 錨鎖 byōsa

port (harbor) 港 minato
berth, wharf 埠頭 futō
to berth (moor) 係留する keiryū suru
to cast off 出航する shukkō suru

trip, voyage 旅行 ryokō
cruise (sea trip) クルーズ kurūzu
course (route) 針路 shinro
route (itinerary) 船のルート fune no rūto

fairway 航路 kōro
shallows (shoal) 浅瀬 asase
to run aground 浅瀬に乗り上げる asase ni noriageru

storm 嵐 arashi
signal 信号 shingō
to sink (vi) 沈没する chinbotsu suru
Man overboard! 落水したぞ！ ochimizu shi ta zo!
SOS SOS

ring buoy 救命浮輪 kyūmei ukiwa

144.

air-traffic controller	航空管制官	kōkū kansei kan
departure	出発	shuppatsu
arrival	到着	tōchaku
to arrive (by plane)	到着する	tōchaku suru
departure time	出発時刻	shuppatsu jikoku
arrival time	到着時刻	tōchaku jikoku
to be delayed	遅れる	okureru
flight delay	フライトの遅延	furaito no chien
information board	フライト情報	furaito jōhō
information	案内	annai
to announce (vt)	アナウンスする	anaunsu suru
flight (e.g., next ~)	フライト	furaito
customs	税関	zeikan
customs officer	税関吏	zeikanri
customs declaration	税関申告	zeikan shinkoku
to fill out (vt)	記入する	kinyū suru
to fill out the declaration	申告書を記入する	shinkoku sho wo kinyū suru
passport control	入国審査	nyūkoku shinsa
luggage	荷物	nimotsu
hand luggage	持ち込み荷物	mochikomi nimotsu
Lost Luggage Desk	荷物紛失窓口	nimotsu funshitsu madoguchi
luggage cart	荷物カート	nimotsu kāto
landing	着陸	chakuriku
landing strip	滑走路	kassō ro
to land (vi)	着陸する	chakuriku suru
airstairs	タラップ	tarappu
check-in	チェックイン	chekkuin
check-in desk	チェックインカウンター	chekkuin kauntā
to check-in (vi)	チェックインする	chekkuin suru
boarding pass	搭乗券	tōjō ken
departure gate	出発ゲート	shuppatsu gēto
transit	乗り継ぎ	noritsugi
to wait (vt)	待つ	matsu
departure lounge	出発ロビー	shuppatsu robī
to see off	見送る	miokuru
to say goodbye	別れを告げる	wakare wo tsugeru

145.

motorcycle, bike	オートバイ	ōtobai
to go by bicycle	自転車で行く	jitensha de iku
handlebars	ハンドル	handoru
pedal	ペダル	pedaru
brakes	ブレーキ	burēki
bicycle seat	サドル	sadoru
pump	ポンプ	ponpu
luggage rack	荷台	nidai
front lamp	ヘッドライト	heddoraito
helmet	ヘルメット	herumetto
wheel	車輪	sharin
fender	泥除け	doroyoke
rim	リム	rimu
spoke	スポーク	supōku

door handle	ドアノブ	doa nobu
door lock	ドアロック	doa rokku
license plate	ナンバープレート	nanbā purēto
muffler	消音器	shōon ki
gas tank	ガソリンタンク	gasorin tanku
tail pipe	排気管	haiki kan
gas, accelerator	アクセル	akuseru
pedal	ペダル	pedaru
gas pedal	アクセルペダル	akuseru pedaru
brake	ブレーキ	burēki
brake pedal	ブレーキペダル	burēki pedaru
to slow down (to brake)	ブレーキをかける	burēki wo kakeru
parking brake	パーキングブレーキ	pākingu burēki
clutch	クラッチ	kuracchi
clutch pedal	クラッチペダル	kuracchi pedaru
clutch plate	クラッチディスク	kuracchi disuku
shock absorber	ショックアブソーバー	shokku abusōbā
wheel	車輪	sharin
spare tire	スペアタイヤ	supea taiya
tire	タイヤ	taiya
hubcap	ホイールキャップ	hoīru kyappu
driving wheels	駆動輪	kudō wa
front-wheel drive (as adj)	前輪駆動の	zenrin kudō no
rear-wheel drive (as adj)	後輪駆動の	kōrin kudō no
all-wheel drive (as adj)	四輪駆動の	yonrin kudō no
gearbox	ギアボックス	gia bokkusu
automatic (adj)	オートマチックの	ōtomachikku no
mechanical (adj)	マニュアルの	manyuaru no
gear shift	シフトレバー	shifuto rebā
headlight	ヘッドライト	heddoraito
headlights	ヘッドライト	heddoraito
low beam	ロービーム	rō bīmu
high beam	ハイビーム	hai bīmu
brake light	ブレーキライト	burēki raito
parking lights	パーキングライト	pākingu raito
hazard lights	ハザードランプ	hazādo ranpu
fog lights	フォグランプ	fogu ranpu
turn signal	方向指示器	hōkō shiji ki
back-up light	バックライト	bakku raito

148.

piston	ピストン	pisuton
cylinder	シリンダー	shirindā
valve	バルブ	barubu
injector	インジェクター	injekutā
generator	オルタネーター	orutanētā
carburetor	キャブレター	kyaburetā
engine oil	エンジンオイル	enjin oiru
radiator	ラジエーター	rajiētā
coolant	クーラント	kūranto
cooling fan	冷却ファン	reikyaku fan
battery (accumulator)	バッテリー	batterī
starter	スターター	sutātā
ignition	点火	tenka
spark plug	スパークプラグ	supāku puragu
terminal (of battery)	端子	tanshi
positive terminal	プラス端子	purasu tanshi
negative terminal	マイナス端子	mainasu tanshi
fuse	ヒューズ	hyūzu
air filter	エアーフィルター	eā firutā
oil filter	オイルフィルター	oiru firutā
fuel filter	燃料フィルター	nenryō firutā

150.

bolt (with nut)	ボルト	boruto
screw bolt (without nut)	ネジ [ねじ]	neji
nut	ナット	natto
washer	ワッシャー	wasshā
bearing	軸受け	jikuuke
tube	チューブ	chūbu
gasket (head ~)	ガスケット	gasu ketto
cable, wire	ワイヤー	waiyā
jack	ジャッキ	jakki
wrench	スパナ	supana
hammer	金槌 [金づち]	kanazuchi
pump	ポンプ	ponpu
screwdriver	ドライバー	doraibā
fire extinguisher	消火器	shōka ki
warning triangle	三角表示板	sankaku hyōji ban
to stall (vi)	エンストする	ensuto suru
stalling	エンスト	ensuto
to be broken	壊れる	kowareru
to overheat (vi)	オーバーヒートする	ōbāhīto suru
to be clogged up	詰まっている	tsumatte iru
to freeze up (pipes, etc.)	氷結する	hyōketsu suru
to burst (vi, ab. tube)	爆発する	bakuhatsu suru
pressure	空気圧	kūkiatsu
level	残量	zan ryō
slack (~ belt)	たるんだ	tarun da
dent	へこみ	hekomi
abnormal noise (motor)	ノッキング	nokkingu
crack	ひび	hibi
scratch	擦り傷	surikizu

151.

gas station	ガソリンスタンド	gasorin sutando
parking lot	駐車場	chūsha jō
gas pump	給油ポンプ	kyūyu ponpu
auto repair shop	修理工場	shūri kōjō
to get gas	給油する	kyūyu suru
fuel	燃料	nenryō
jerrycan	ジェリカン	jerikan
asphalt	アスファルト	asufaruto
road markings	道路標示	dōro hyōji
curb	縁石	enseki
guardrail	ガードレール	gādorēru
ditch	側溝	sokkō
roadside (shoulder)	路肩	rokata
lamppost	街灯柱	gaitō bashira
to drive (a car)	運転する	unten suru
to turn (~ to the left)	曲がる	magaru
to make a U-turn	Uターンする	yūtān suru
reverse (~ gear)	バック	bakku
to honk (vi)	クラクションを鳴らす	kurakushon wo narasu
honk (sound)	クラクション	kurakushon
to get stuck	抜け出せなくなる	nukedase naku naru
to spin (in mud)	ホイールスピンする	hoīru supin suru
to cut, to turn off	止める	tomeru
speed	スピード	supīdo
to exceed the speed limit	スピード違反をする	supīdo ihan wo suru
to give a ticket	交通違反切符を渡す	kōtsū ihan kippu wo watasu
traffic lights	信号	shingō
driver's license	運転免許証	unten menkyo shō
grade crossing	踏切	fumikiri
intersection	交差点	kōsaten
crosswalk	横断歩道	ōdan hodō
bend, curve	カーブ	kābu
pedestrian zone	歩行者専用区域	hokō sha senyō kuiki

to receive gifts	プレゼントをもらう	purezento wo morau
bouquet (of flowers)	花束	hanataba
congratulations	祝辞	shukuji
to congratulate (vt)	祝う	iwau
greeting card	グリーティングカード	gurītingu kādo
to send a postcard	はがきを送る	hagaki wo okuru
to get a postcard	はがきを受け取る	hagaki wo uketoru
toast	祝杯	shukuhai
to offer (a drink, etc.)	…に一杯おごる	… ni ippai ogoru
champagne	シャンパン	shanpan
to have fun	楽しむ	tanoshimu
fun, merriment	歓楽	kanraku
joy (emotion)	喜び	yorokobi
dance	ダンス	dansu
to dance (vi, vt)	踊る	odoru
waltz	ワルツ	warutsu
tango	タンゴ	tango

153.

obituary	死亡記事	shibō kiji
to cry (weep)	泣く	naku
to sob (vi)	むせび泣く	musebinaku

154.

to betray (vt)	裏切る	uragiru
deserter	脱走兵	dassō hei
to desert (vi)	脱走する	dassō suru
mercenary	傭兵	yōhei
recruit	新兵	shinpei
volunteer	志願兵	shigan hei
dead (n)	死者	shisha
wounded (n)	負傷者	fushō sha
prisoner of war	捕虜	horyo

155.

siege (to be under ~)	包囲	hōi
offensive (n)	攻勢	kōsei
to go on the offensive	攻勢に出る	kōsei ni deru
retreat	撤退	tettai
to retreat (vi)	撤退する	tettai suru
encirclement	包囲	hōi
to encircle (vt)	包囲する	hōi suru
bombing (by aircraft)	爆撃	bakugeki
to drop a bomb	爆弾を投下する	bakudan wo tōka suru
to bomb (vt)	爆撃する	bakugeki suru
explosion	爆発	bakuhatsu
shot	発砲	happō
to fire a shot	発砲する	happō suru
firing (burst of ~)	砲火	hōka
to take aim (at …)	狙う	nerau
to point (a gun)	向ける	mukeru
to hit (the target)	命中する	meichū suru
to sink (~ a ship)	撃沈する	gekichin suru
hole (in a ship)	穴	ana
to founder, to sink (vi)	沈没する	chinbotsu suru
front (war ~)	戦線	sensen
rear (homefront)	銃後	jūgo
evacuation	避難	hinan
to evacuate (vt)	避難する	hinan suru
trench	塹壕	zangō
barbwire	有刺鉄線	yūshitessen
barrier (anti tank ~)	障害物	shōgai butsu
watchtower	監視塔	kanshi tō
hospital	軍病院	gun byōin
to wound (vt)	負傷させる	fushō saseru
wound	負傷	fushō
wounded (n)	負傷者	fushō sha
to be wounded	負傷する	fushō suru
serious (wound)	重い	omoi

156.

chemical weapons	化学兵器	kagaku heiki
nuclear (adj)	核…	kaku …
nuclear weapons	核兵器	kakuheiki
bomb	爆弾	bakudan
atomic bomb	原子爆弾	genshi bakudan
pistol (gun)	拳銃、ピストル	kenjū, pisutoru
rifle	ライフル	raifuru
submachine gun	サブマシンガン	sabumashin gan
machine gun	マシンガン	mashin gan
muzzle	銃口	jūkō
barrel	砲身	hōshin
caliber	口径	kōkei
trigger	トリガー	torigā
sight (aiming device)	照準器	shōjun ki
magazine	弾倉	dansō
butt (of rifle)	台尻	daijiri
hand grenade	手榴弾	shuryūdan
explosive	爆発物	bakuhatsu butsu
bullet	弾	tama
cartridge	実弾	jitsudan
charge	装薬	sō yaku
ammunition	弾薬	danyaku
bomber (aircraft)	爆撃機	bakugeki ki
fighter	戦闘機	sentō ki
helicopter	ヘリコプター	herikoputā
anti-aircraft gun	対空砲	taikū hō
tank	戦車	sensha
tank gun	戦車砲	sensha hō
artillery	砲兵	hōhei
cannon	大砲	taihō
to lay (a gun)	狙いを定める	nerai wo sadameru
shell (projectile)	砲弾	hōdan
mortar bomb	迫撃砲弾	hakugeki hō dan
mortar	迫撃砲	hakugeki hō
splinter (shell fragment)	砲弾の破片	hōdan no hahen
submarine	潜水艦	sensui kan
torpedo	魚雷	gyorai
missile	ミサイル	misairu
to load (gun)	装填する	sōten suru
to shoot (vi)	撃つ	utsu

to point at (the cannon)	向ける	mukeru
bayonet	銃剣	jūken
epee	エペ	epe
saber (e.g., cavalry ~)	サーベル	sāberu
spear (weapon)	槍	yari
bow	弓	yumi
arrow	矢	ya
musket	マスケット銃	masuketto jū
crossbow	石弓	ishiyumi

157.

archeological (adj)	考古学の	kōkogaku no
excavation site	発掘現場	hakkutsu genba
excavations	発掘	hakkutsu
find (object)	発見	hakken
fragment	一片	ippen

158.

territory	領土	ryōdo
to attack (invade)	攻撃する	kōgeki suru
to conquer (vt)	征服する	seifuku suru
to occupy (invade)	占領する	senryō suru
siege (to be under ~)	包囲	hōi
besieged (adj)	攻囲された	kōi sare ta
to besiege (vt)	攻囲する	kōi suru
inquisition	宗教裁判	shūkyō saiban
inquisitor	宗教裁判官	shūkyō saibankan
torture	拷問	gōmon
cruel (adj)	残酷な	zankoku na
heretic	異端者	itan sha
heresy	異端	itan
seafaring	船旅	funatabi
pirate	海賊	kaizoku
piracy	海賊行為	kaizoku kōi
boarding (attack)	移乗攻撃	ijō kōgeki
loot, booty	戦利品	senri hin
treasures	宝	takara
discovery	発見	hakken
to discover (new land, etc.)	発見する	hakken suru
expedition	探検	tanken
musketeer	銃士	jū shi
cardinal	枢機卿	sūkikyō
heraldry	紋章学	monshō gaku
heraldic (adj)	紋章の	monshō no

159.

magnate	マグナート	magunāto
director	責任者	sekinin sha
chief	長	chō
manager (director)	管理者	kanri sha
boss	ボス	bosu
owner	経営者	keieisha
leader	リーダー	rīdā
head (~ of delegation)	長	chō
authorities	当局	tōkyoku
superiors	上司	jōshi
governor	知事	chiji
consul	領事	ryōji
diplomat	外交官	gaikō kan
mayor	市長	shichō
sheriff	保安官	hoan kan
emperor	皇帝	kōtei
tsar, czar	ツァーリ	tsāri
pharaoh	ファラオ	farao
khan	ハン	han

160.

murder	殺人	satsujin
murderer	殺人者	satsujin sha
gunshot	発砲	happō
to fire a shot	発砲する	happō suru
to shoot to death	射殺する	shasatsu suru
to shoot (vi)	撃つ	utsu
shooting	射撃	shageki
incident (fight, etc.)	事件	jiken
fight, brawl	喧嘩	kenka
Help!	助けて！	tasuke te!
victim	被害者	higai sha
to damage (vt)	損害を与える	songai wo ataeru
damage	損害	songai
dead body	死体	shitai
grave (~ crime)	重い	omoi
to attack (vt)	攻撃する	kōgeki suru
to beat (dog, person)	殴る	naguru
to beat up	打ちのめす	uchinomesu
to take (rob of sth)	強奪する	gōdatsu suru
to stab to death	刺し殺す	sashikorosu
to maim (vt)	重症を負わせる	jūshō wo owaseru
to wound (vt)	負わせる	owaseru
blackmail	恐喝	kyōkatsu
to blackmail (vt)	恐喝する	kyōkatsu suru
blackmailer	恐喝者	kyōkatsu sha
protection racket	ゆすり	yusuri
racketeer	ゆすりを働く人	yusuri wo hataraku hito
gangster	暴力団員	bōryokudan in
mafia, Mob	マフィア	mafia
pickpocket	すり	suri
burglar	強盗	gōtō
smuggling	密輸	mitsuyu
smuggler	密輸者	mitsuyu sha
forgery	偽造	gizō
to forge (counterfeit)	偽造する	gizō suru
fake (forged)	偽造の	gizō no

161.

maniac	マニア	mania
prostitute (fem.)	売春婦	baishun fu
prostitution	売春	baishun
pimp	ポン引き	pon biki
drug addict	麻薬中毒者	mayaku chūdoku sha
drug dealer	麻薬の売人	mayaku no bainin
to blow up (bomb)	爆発させる	bakuhatsu saseru
explosion	爆発	bakuhatsu
to set fire	放火する	hōka suru
incendiary (arsonist)	放火犯人	hōka hannin
terrorism	テロリズム	terorizumu
terrorist	テロリスト	terorisuto
hostage	人質	hitojichi
to swindle (vt)	詐欺を働く	sagi wo hataraku
swindle	詐欺	sagi
swindler	詐欺師	sagi shi
to bribe (vt)	賄賂を渡す	wairo wo watasu
bribery	賄賂の授受	wairo no juju
bribe	賄賂	wairo
poison	毒	doku
to poison (vt)	…を毒殺する	… wo dokusatsu suru
to poison oneself	毒薬を飲む	dokuyaku wo nomu
suicide (act)	自殺	jisatsu
suicide (person)	自殺者	jisatsu sha
to threaten (vt)	脅す	odosu
threat	脅し	odoshi
to make an attempt	殺そうとする	koroso u to suru
attempt (attack)	殺人未遂	satsujin misui
to steal (a car)	盗む	nusumu
to hijack (a plane)	ハイジャックする	haijakku suru
revenge	復讐	fukushū
to revenge (vt)	復讐する	fukushū suru
to torture (vt)	拷問する	gōmon suru
torture	拷問	gōmon
to torment (vt)	虐待する	gyakutai suru
pirate	海賊	kaizoku
hooligan	フーリガン	fūrigan
armed (adj)	武装した	busō shi ta
violence	暴力	bōryoku
illegal (unlawful)	違法な	ihō na

spying (n)	スパイ行為	supai kōi
to spy (vi)	スパイする	supai suru

162.

amnesty	恩赦	onsha
police	警察	keisatsu
police officer	警官	keikan
police station	警察署	keisatsu sho
billy club	警棒	keibō
bullhorn	拡声器	kakusei ki
patrol car	パトロールカー	patorōrukā
siren	サイレン	sairen
to turn on the siren	サイレンを鳴らす	sairen wo narasu
siren call	サイレンの音	sairen no oto
crime scene	犯行現場	hankō genba
witness	目撃者	mokugeki sha
freedom	自由	jiyū
accomplice	共犯者	kyōhan sha
to flee (vi)	逃走する	tōsō suru
trace (to leave a ~)	形跡	keiseki

163.

document	文書	bunsho
proof (evidence)	証拠	shōko
to prove (vt)	証明する	shōmei suru
footprint	足跡	ashiato
fingerprints	指紋	shimon
piece of evidence	一つの証拠	hitotsu no shōko
alibi	アリバイ	aribai
innocent (not guilty)	無罪の	muzai no
injustice	不当	futō
unjust, unfair (adj)	不当な	futō na
criminal (adj)	犯罪の	hanzai no
to confiscate (vt)	没収する	bosshū suru
drug (illegal substance)	麻薬	mayaku
weapon, gun	兵器	heiki
to disarm (vt)	武装解除する	busō kaijo suru
to order (command)	命令する	meirei suru
to disappear (vi)	姿を消す	sugata wo kesu
law	法律	hōritsu
legal, lawful (adj)	合法の	gōhō no
illegal, illicit (adj)	違法な	ihō na
responsibility (blame)	責め	seme
responsible (adj)	責めを負うべき	seme wo ō beki

North Star	北極星	hokkyokusei
Martian	火星人	kasei jin
extraterrestrial (n)	宇宙人	uchū jin
alien	異星人	i hoshi jin
flying saucer	空飛ぶ円盤	sora tobu enban
spaceship	宇宙船	uchūsen
space station	宇宙ステーション	uchū sutēshon
blast-off	打ち上げ	uchiage
engine	エンジン	enjin
nozzle	ノズル	nozuru
fuel	燃料	nenryō
cockpit, flight deck	コックピット	kokkupitto
antenna	アンテナ	antena
porthole	舷窓	gensō
solar battery	太陽電池	taiyō denchi
spacesuit	宇宙服	uchū fuku
weightlessness	無重力	mu jūryoku
oxygen	酸素	sanso
docking (in space)	ドッキング	dokkingu
to dock (vi, vt)	ドッキングする	dokkingu suru
observatory	天文台	tenmondai
telescope	望遠鏡	bōenkyō
to observe (vt)	観察する	kansatsu suru
to explore (vt)	探索する	tansaku suru

165.

North America	北アメリカ	kita amerika
South America	南アメリカ	minami amerika
Antarctica	南極大陸	nankyokutairiku
the Arctic	北極	hokkyoku

166.

coral	サンゴ	sango
coral reef	サンゴ礁	sangoshō
deep (adj)	深い	fukai
depth (deep water)	深さ	fuka sa
abyss	深淵	shinen
trench (e.g., Mariana ~)	海溝	kaikō
current, stream	海流	kairyū
to surround (bathe)	取り囲む	torikakomu
shore	海岸	kaigan
coast	沿岸	engan
high tide	満潮	manchō
low tide	干潮	kanchō
sandbank	砂州	sasu
bottom	底	soko
wave	波	nami
crest (~ of a wave)	波頭	namigashira
froth (foam)	泡	awa
storm	嵐	arashi
hurricane	ハリケーン	harikēn
tsunami	津波	tsunami
calm (dead ~)	凪	nagi
quiet, calm (adj)	穏やかな	odayaka na
pole	極地	kyokuchi
polar (adj)	極地の	kyokuchi no
latitude	緯度	ido
longitude	経度	keido
parallel	度線	dosen
equator	赤道	sekidō
sky	空	sora
horizon	地平線	chiheisen
air	空気	kūki
lighthouse	灯台	tōdai
to dive (vi)	飛び込む	tobikomu
to sink (ab. boat)	沈没する	chinbotsu suru
treasures	宝	takara

168.

mountain ridge	山稜	sanryō
summit, top	頂上	chōjō
peak	とがった山頂	togatta sanchō
foot (of mountain)	麓	fumoto
slope (mountainside)	山腹	sanpuku
volcano	火山	kazan
active volcano	活火山	kakkazan
dormant volcano	休火山	kyūkazan
eruption	噴火	funka
crater	噴火口	funkakō
magma	岩漿、マグマ	ganshō, maguma
lava	溶岩	yōgan
molten (~ lava)	溶…	yō …
canyon	峡谷	kyōkoku
gorge	峡谷	kyōkoku
crevice	裂け目	sakeme
abyss (chasm)	奈落の底	naraku no soko
pass, col	峠	tōge
plateau	高原	kōgen
cliff	断崖	dangai
hill	丘	oka
glacier	氷河	hyōga
waterfall	滝	taki
geyser	間欠泉	kanketsusen
lake	湖	mizūmi
plain	平原	heigen
landscape	風景	fūkei
echo	こだま	kodama
alpinist	登山家	tozan ka
rock climber	ロッククライマー	rokku kuraimā
to conquer (in climbing)	征服する	seifuku suru
climb (an easy ~)	登山	tozan

169.

current, stream	流れ	nagare
downstream (adv)	下流の	karyū no
upstream (adv)	上流の	jōryū no
inundation	洪水	kōzui
flooding	氾濫	hanran
to overflow (vi)	氾濫する	hanran suru
to flood (vt)	水浸しにする	mizubitashi ni suru
shallows (shoal)	浅瀬	asase
rapids	急流	kyūryū
dam	ダム	damu
canal	運河	unga
artificial lake	ため池 [溜池]	tameike
sluice, lock	水門	suimon
water body (pond, etc.)	水域	suīki
swamp, bog	沼地	numachi
marsh	湿地	shicchi
whirlpool	渦	uzu
stream (brook)	小川	ogawa
drinking (ab. water)	飲用の	inyō no
fresh (~ water)	淡…	tan …
ice	氷	kōri
to freeze (ab. river, etc.)	氷結する	hyōketsu suru

170.

top (of the tree)	木のてっぺん	kinoteppen
branch	枝	eda
bough	主枝	shushi
bud (on shrub, tree)	芽［め］	me
needle (of pine tree)	松葉	matsuba
pine cone	松ぼっくり	matsubokkuri
hollow (in a tree)	樹洞	kihora
nest	巣	su
burrow (animal hole)	巣穴	su ana
trunk	幹	miki
root	根	ne
bark	樹皮	juhi
moss	コケ［苔］	koke
to uproot (vt)	根こそぎにする	nekosogi ni suru
to chop down	切り倒す	kiritaosu
to deforest (vt)	切り払う	kiriharau
tree stump	切り株	kirikabu
campfire	焚火	takibi
forest fire	森林火災	shinrin kasai
to extinguish (vt)	火を消す	hi wo kesu
forest ranger	森林警備隊員	shinrin keibi taīn
protection	保護	hogo
to protect (~ nature)	保護する	hogo suru
poacher	密漁者	mitsuryō sha
trap (e.g., bear ~)	罠	wana
to pick (mushrooms)	摘み集める	tsumi atsumeru
to pick (berries)	採る	toru
to lose one's way	道に迷う	michi ni mayō

171.

oil (petroleum)	石油	sekiyu
oil pipeline	石油パイプライン	sekiyu paipurain
oil well	油井	yusei
derrick	油井やぐら	yusei ya gura
tanker	タンカー	tankā
sand	砂	suna
limestone	石灰岩	sekkaigan
gravel	砂利	jari
peat	泥炭	deitan
clay	粘土	nendo
coal	石炭	sekitan
iron	鉄	tetsu
gold	金	kin
silver	銀	gin
nickel	ニッケル	nikkeru
copper	銅	dō
zinc	亜鉛	aen
manganese	マンガン	mangan
mercury	水銀	suigin
lead	鉛	namari
mineral	鉱物	kōbutsu
crystal	水晶	suishō
marble	大理石	dairiseki
uranium	ウラン	uran

snow	雪	yuki
it's snowing	雪が降っている	yuki ga futte iru

173.

marten	マツテン	matsu ten
weasel	イタチ（鼬、鼬鼠）	itachi
mink	ミンク	minku
beaver	ビーバー	bībā
otter	カワウソ	kawauso
horse	ウマ［馬］	uma
moose	ヘラジカ（箆鹿）	herajika
deer	シカ［鹿］	shika
camel	ラクダ［駱駝］	rakuda
bison	アメリカバイソン	amerika baison
aurochs	ヨーロッパバイソン	yōroppa baison
buffalo	水牛	suigyū
zebra	シマウマ［縞馬］	shimauma
antelope	レイヨウ	reiyō
roe deer	ノロジカ	noro jika
fallow deer	ダマジカ	damajika
chamois	シャモア	shamoa
wild boar	イノシシ［猪］	inoshishi
whale	クジラ［鯨］	kujira
seal	アザラシ	azarashi
walrus	セイウチ［海象］	seiuchi
fur seal	オットセイ［膃肭臍］	ottosei
dolphin	いるか［海豚］	iruka
bear	クマ［熊］	kuma
polar bear	ホッキョクグマ	hokkyokuguma
panda	パンダ	panda
monkey	サル［猿］	saru
chimpanzee	チンパンジー	chinpanjī
orangutan	オランウータン	oranwutan
gorilla	ゴリラ	gorira
macaque	マカク	makaku
gibbon	テナガザル	tenagazaru
elephant	ゾウ［象］	zō
rhinoceros	サイ［犀］	sai
giraffe	キリン	kirin
hippopotamus	カバ［河馬］	kaba
kangaroo	カンガルー	kangarū
koala (bear)	コアラ	koara
mongoose	マングース	mangūsu
chinchilla	チンチラ	chinchira
skunk	スカンク	sukanku
porcupine	ヤマアラシ	yamārashi

176.

177.

179.

wood grouse	ヨーロッパ オオライチョウ	yōroppa ōraichō
black grouse	クロライチョウ	kuro raichō
partridge	ヨーロッパヤマウズラ	yōroppa yamauzura
starling	ムクドリ	mukudori
canary	カナリア [金糸雀]	kanaria
hazel grouse	エゾライチョウ	ezo raichō
chaffinch	ズアオアトリ	zuaoatori
bullfinch	ウソ [鷽]	uso
seagull	カモメ [鴎]	kamome
albatross	アホウドリ	ahōdori
penguin	ペンギン	pengin

180.

trout	マス [鱒]	masu
eel	ウナギ [鰻]	unagi
electric ray	シビレエイ	shibireei
moray eel	ウツボ [鱓]	utsubo
piranha	ピラニア	pirania
shark	サメ [鮫]	same
dolphin	イルカ [海豚]	iruka
whale	クジラ [鯨]	kujira
crab	カニ [蟹]	kani
jellyfish	クラゲ [水母]	kurage
octopus	タコ [蛸]	tako
starfish	ヒトデ [海星]	hitode
sea urchin	ウニ [海胆]	uni
seahorse	タツノオトシゴ	tatsunootoshigo
oyster	カキ [牡蠣]	kaki
shrimp	エビ	ebi
lobster	イセエビ	iseebi
spiny lobster	スパイニーロブスター	supainī robusutā

182.

183.

larva	幼虫	yōchū
fin	ひれ［鰭］	hire
scales (of fish, reptile)	鱗（うろこ）	uroko
fang (canine)	犬歯	kenshi
paw (e.g., cat's ~)	足	ashi
muzzle (snout)	鼻口部	hana guchi bu
mouth (of cat, dog)	口	kuchi
tail	尻尾	shippo
whiskers	洞毛	dōmo u
hoof	ひづめ	hizume
horn	角	tsuno
carapace	甲羅	kōra
shell (of mollusk)	貝殻	kaigara
eggshell	卵の殻	tamago no kara
animal's hair (pelage)	毛	ke
pelt (hide)	毛皮	kegawa

185.

hollow (in a tree)	樹洞	kihora
burrow (animal hole)	巣穴	su ana
anthill	アリ塚［蟻塚］	arizuka

187.

pear	洋梨	yōnashi
plum	プラム	puramu
strawberry	イチゴ（苺）	ichigo
cherry	チェリー	cherī
sour cherry	サワー チェリー	sawā cherī
sweet cherry	スイート チェリー	suīto cherī
grape	ブドウ［葡萄］	budō
raspberry	ラズベリー（木苺）	razuberī
blackcurrant	クロスグリ	kuro suguri
redcurrant	フサスグリ	fusa suguri
gooseberry	セイヨウスグリ	seiyō suguri
cranberry	クランベリー	kuranberī
orange	オレンジ	orenji
mandarin	マンダリン	mandarin
pineapple	パイナップル	painappuru
banana	バナナ	banana
date	デーツ	dētsu
lemon	レモン	remon
apricot	アンズ［杏子］	anzu
peach	モモ［桃］	momo
kiwi	キウイ	kiui
grapefruit	グレープフルーツ	gurēbu furūtsu
berry	ベリー	berī
berries	ベリー	berī
cowberry	コケモモ	kokemomo
field strawberry	ノイチゴ［野いちご］	noichigo
bilberry	ビルベリー	biruberī

190.

rubber plant, ficus	イチジク	ichijiku
lily	ユリ［百合］	yuri
geranium	ゼラニウム	zeranyūmu
hyacinth	ヒヤシンス	hiyashinsu
mimosa	ミモザ	mimoza
narcissus	スイセン［水仙］	suisen
nasturtium	キンレンカ［金蓮花］	kinrenka
orchid	ラン［蘭］	ran
peony	シャクヤク［芍薬］	shakuyaku
violet	スミレ［菫］	sumire
pansy	パンジー	panjī
forget-me-not	ワスレナグサ［勿忘草］	wasurenagusa
daisy	デイジー	deijī
poppy	ポピー	popī
hemp	アサ［麻］	asa
mint	ミント	minto
lily of the valley	スズラン［鈴蘭］	suzuran
snowdrop	スノードロップ	sunōdoroppu
nettle	イラクサ［刺草］	irakusa
sorrel	スイバ	suiba
water lily	スイレン［睡蓮］	suiren
fern	シダ	shida
lichen	地衣類	chī rui
tropical greenhouse	温室	onshitsu
grass lawn	芝生	shibafu
flowerbed	花壇	kadan
plant	植物	shokubutsu
grass, herb	草	kusa
blade of grass	草の葉	kusa no ha
leaf	葉	ha
petal	花びら	hanabira
stem	茎	kuki
tuber	塊茎	kaikei
young plant (shoot)	シュート	shūto
thorn	茎針	kuki hari
to blossom (vi)	開花する	kaika suru
to fade, to wither	しおれる	shioreru
smell (odor)	香り	kaori
to cut (flowers)	切る	kiru
to pick (a flower)	摘む	tsumamu

191.

poll, elections	選挙	senkyo
to elect (vt)	選出する	senshutsu suru
elector, voter	投票者	tōhyō sha
election campaign	選挙戦	senkyo sen
voting (n)	投票	tōhyō
to vote (vi)	投票する	tōhyō suru
suffrage, right to vote	投票権	tōhyō ken
candidate	候補者	kōho sha
to be a candidate	選挙に出る	senkyo ni deru
campaign	運動	undō
opposition (as adj)	野党の	yatō no
opposition (n)	野党	yatō
visit	訪問	hōmon
official visit	公式訪問	kōshiki hōmon
international (adj)	国際的な	kokusai teki na
negotiations	交渉	kōshō
to negotiate (vi)	交渉する	kōshō suru

193.

conspiracy (plot)	陰謀	inbō
provocation	挑発	chōhatsu
to overthrow (regime, etc.)	打倒する	datō suru
overthrow (of government)	打倒	datō
revolution	革命	kakumei
coup d'état	クーデター	kūdetā
military coup	軍事クーデター	gunji kūdetā
crisis	危機	kiki
economic recession	不景気	fukeiki
demonstrator (protester)	デモ参加者	demo sanka sha
demonstration	デモ	demo
martial law	戒厳令	kaigen rei
military base	軍事基地	gunji kichi
stability	安定性	antei sei
stable (adj)	安定した	antei shi ta
exploitation	搾取	sakushu
to exploit (workers)	搾取する	sakushu suru
racism	人種差別	jinshu sabetsu
racist	人種差別主義者	jinshu sabetsu shugi sha
fascism	ファシズム	fashizumu
fascist	ファシスト	fashisuto

194.

population	人口	jinkō
people (a lot of ~)	人々	hitobito
nation (people)	民族	minzoku
generation	世代	sedai
territory (area)	領域	ryōiki
region	地域	chīki
state (part of a country)	州	shū
tradition	慣習	kanshū
custom (tradition)	風習	fūshū
ecology	エコロジー	ekorojī
Indian (Native American)	インディアン	indian
Gipsy (masc.)	ジプシー	jipushī
Gipsy (fem.)	ジプシー	jipushī
Gipsy (adj)	ジプシーの	jipushī no
empire	帝国	teikoku
colony	植民地	shokumin chi
slavery	奴隷制度	dorei seido
invasion	侵略	shinrya ku
famine	飢餓	kiga

195.

Orthodox	正教の	seikyō no
Presbyterianism	長老派	chōrō ha
Presbyterian Church	長老派教会	chōrō ha kyōkai
Presbyterian (n)	長老派教会員	chōrō ha kyōkaīn
Lutheranism	ルーテル教会	rūteru kyōkai
Lutheran (n)	ルーテル教徒	rūteru kyōto
Baptist Church	バプテスト教会	baputesuto kyōkai
Baptist (n)	バプテスト	baputesuto
Anglican Church	英国国教会	eikoku kokkyōkai
Anglican (n)	英国国教徒	eikoku koku kyōto
Mormonism	モルモン教	morumon kyō
Mormon (n)	モルモン教徒	morumon kyōto
Judaism	ユダヤ教	yudaya kyō
Jew (n)	ユダヤ教徒	yudaya kyōto
Buddhism	仏教	bukkyō
Buddhist (n)	仏教徒	bukkyōto
Hinduism	ヒンドゥー教	hindū kyō
Hindu (n)	ヒンドゥー教徒	hindū kyōto
Islam	イスラム教	isuramukyō
Muslim (n)	イスラム教徒	isuramu kyōto
Muslim (adj)	イスラム教の	isuramu kyō no
Shiah Islam	シーア派	shīaha
Shiite (n)	シーア派	shīaha
Sunni Islam	スンニ派	sunniha
Sunnite (n)	スンニ派	sunniha

196.

parishioners	教区民	kyō kumin
believer	信者	shinja
atheist	無神論者	mushin ron sha

197.

Commandment	戒律	kairitsu
prophet	預言者	yogen sha
prophecy	預言	yogen
Allah	アッラー	arrā
Mohammed	マホメット	mahometto
the Koran	コーラン	kōran
mosque	モスク	mosuku
mullah	ムッラー	murrā
prayer	祈り	inori
to pray (vi, vt)	祈る	inoru
pilgrimage	巡礼	junrei
pilgrim	巡礼者	junrei sha
Mecca	メッカ	mekka
church	教会堂	kyōkaidō
temple	寺院	jīn
cathedral	大聖堂	dai seidō
Gothic (adj)	ゴシック…	goshikku …
synagogue	シナゴーグ	shinagōgu
mosque	モスク	mosuku
chapel	チャペル	chaperu
abbey	修道院	shūdōin
convent	女子修道院	joshi shūdōin
monastery	男子修道院	danshi shūdōin
bell (in church)	鐘	kane
bell tower	鐘楼	shurō
to ring (ab. bells)	鳴る	naru
cross	十字架	jūjika
cupola (roof)	ドーム	dōmu
icon	イコン	ikon
soul	魂	tamashī
fate (destiny)	運命	unmei
evil (n)	悪	aku
good (n)	善	zen
vampire	吸血鬼	kyūketsuki
witch (sorceress)	魔女	majo
demon	悪魔	akuma
devil	鬼	oni
spirit	精神	seishin
redemption (giving us ~)	贖罪	shokuzai
to redeem (vt)	罪を贖う	tsumi wo aganau
church service, mass	ミサ	misa
to say mass	ミサを行う	misa wo okonau

confession	告解	kokkai
to confess (vi)	告解する	kokkai suru
saint (n)	聖人	seijin
sacred (holy)	神聖な	shinsei na
holy water	聖水	seisui
ritual (n)	儀式	gishiki
ritual (adj)	儀式の	gishiki no
sacrifice	犠牲	gisei
superstition	迷信	meishin
superstitious (adj)	縁起を担ぐ	engi wo katsugu
afterlife	来世	raise
eternal life	永遠の生命	eien no seimei

position	位置	ichi
principle	原理	genri
problem	問題	mondai
process	一連の作業	ichiren no sagyō
progress	進歩	shinpo
property (quality)	性質	seishitsu
reaction	反応	hannō
risk	危険	kiken
secret	秘密	himitsu
section (sector)	セクション	sekushon
series	シリーズ	shirīzu
shape (outer form)	形状	keijō
situation	状況	jōkyō
solution	解決	kaiketsu
standard (adj)	標準の	hyōjun no
standard (level of quality)	標準	hyōjun
stop (pause)	休止	kyūshi
style	スタイル	sutairu
system	システム	shisutemu
table (chart)	表	hyō
tempo, rate	テンポ	tenpo
term (word, expression)	用語	yōgo
thing (object, item)	物	mono
truth	真実	shinjitsu
turn (please wait your ~)	順番	junban
type (sort, kind)	型	gata
urgent (adj)	至急の	shikyū no
urgently (adv)	至急に	shikyū ni
utility (usefulness)	実用性	jitsuyō sei
variant (alternative)	バリアント	barianto
way (means, method)	方法	hōhō
zone	地帯	chitai

CPSIA information can be obtained
at www.ICGtesting.com
Printed in the USA
LVOW04s2312260716
497924LV00027B/602/P